WRITE SOURCE
SkillsBook
EDITING AND PROOFREADING PRACTICE

a resource of student activities
to accompany
Write Source

WRITE SOURCE®

GREAT SOURCE EDUCATION GROUP
a Houghton Mifflin Company
Wilmington, Massachusetts

A Few Words About the
Write Source SkillsBook

Before you begin . . .

The *SkillsBook* provides you with opportunities to practice the editing and proofreading skills presented in the *Write Source* textbook. The textbook contains guidelines, examples, and models to help you complete your work in the *SkillsBook*.

Each *SkillsBook* activity includes a brief introduction to the topic and refers you to the pages in the textbook that offer additional information and examples. The "Proofreading Activities" focus on punctuation and the mechanics of writing. The "Parts of Speech Activities" highlight each of the eight parts of speech. The "Sentence Activities" provide practice in sentence combining and in correcting common sentence problems.

The Extend

Many activities include an **Extend** at the end of the exercise. Its purpose is to provide ideas for follow-up work that will help you apply what you have learned to your own writing.

Authors: Pat Sebranek and Dave Kemper

CONTENTS

Proofreading Activities

Marking Punctuation

Pretest: Punctuation **3**

END PUNCTUATION

End Punctuation **5**
Review: End Punctuation **6**

COMMAS

Commas Between Independent Clauses **7**
Commas in a Series & to Separate Equal Adjectives **8**
Commas After Introductory Phrases & Clauses **9**
Review: Commas 1 **11**
Commas to Set Off Contrasted Elements & Appositives **12**
Other Uses of Commas **13**
Commas with Nonrestrictive Phrases & Clauses 1 and 2 **14**
Review: Commas 2 **16**

SEMICOLONS & COLONS

Semicolons to Join Independent Clauses **17**
Semicolons to Separate Word Groups Containing Commas **18**
Colons 1 and 2 **19**
Review: Semicolons & Colons **21**

HYPHENS & DASHES

Hyphens 1 and 2 **22**
Dashes **24**
Review: Hyphens & Dashes **25**

APOSTROPHES

Apostrophes to Form Possessives 1, 2, and 3 **26**
Other Uses for Apostrophes **29**
Review: Apostrophes **30**

QUOTATION MARKS & ITALICS (Underlining)

Quotation Marks with Dialogue **31**

Quotation Marks with Direct Quotations **32**

Double & Single Quotation Marks **33**

Italics (Underlining) & Quotation Marks 1 and 2 **34**

Review: Quotation Marks & Italics (Underlining) 36

OTHER FORMS OF PUNCTUATION

Parentheses, Ellipses, and Brackets **38**

Editing for Mechanics

CAPITALIZATION

Pretest: Capitalization **39**

Capitalization 1, 2, and 3 **41**

Review: Capitalization 44

NUMBERS & ABBREVIATIONS

Numbers 1 and 2 **45**

Abbreviations **47**

Review: Numbers & Abbreviations 48

PLURALS & SPELLING

Pretest: Plurals & Spelling **49**

Plurals 1 and 2 **51**

Spelling 1, 2, 3, and 4 **53**

Review: Plurals & Spelling 59

Using the Right Word

Pretest: Using the Right Word **61**

Using the Right Word 1, 2, 3, 4, and 5 **62**

Review: Using the Right Word 67

Proofreading Review 69

Parts of Speech Activities

Nouns

Pretest: Nouns **73**
Types of Nouns **74**
Singular & Plural Nouns **75**
Functions of Nouns **76**
Nominative, Possessive, & Objective Cases of Nouns **77**
Gender of Nouns **78**
Review: Nouns 79

Pronouns

Pretest: Pronouns **80**
Number & Person of Personal Pronouns **81**
Functions of Pronouns **82**
Nominative, Possessive, & Objective Cases of Pronouns **83**
Review: Pronouns 1 84
Relative Pronouns **85**
Indefinite, Interrogative, & Demonstrative Pronouns **86**
Reflexive & Intensive Pronouns **87**
Review: Pronouns 2 88

Verbs

Pretest: Verbs **89**
Types of Main Verbs **90**
Auxiliary (Helping) Verbs **91**
Linking Verbs **92**
Present Tense Verbs & Third-Person Pronouns **93**
Active & Passive Voice **94**
Present, Past, & Future Verb Tenses **95**
Perfect Tense Verbs **96**
Review: Verbs 1 97
Transitive & Intransitive Verbs **98**
Direct & Indirect Objects **99**
Verbals: Gerunds, Infinitives, & Participles **100**
Irregular Verbs 1 and 2 **101**
Verb Moods **103**
Review: Verbs 2 104

Adjectives & Adverbs

Pretest: Adjectives & Adverbs   **105**

Types of Adjectives   **106**

Forms of Adjectives to Compare   **107**

Review: Adjectives   108

Types of Adverbs 1 and 2   **109**

Forms of Adverbs   **111**

Review: Adverbs   112

Prepositions, Conjunctions, & Interjections

Pretest: Prepositions, Conjunctions, & Interjections   **113**

Prepositions & Interjections   **114**

Coordinating Conjunctions   **115**

Correlative Conjunctions   **116**

Subordinating Conjunctions   **117**

Review: Prepositions, Conjunctions, & Interjections   118

Parts of Speech Review   119

Sentence Activities

Sentence Basics

SUBJECTS & PREDICATES

Pretest: Subjects & Predicates **123**
Subjects & Predicates 1 and 2 **124**
Review: Subjects & Predicates 126

PHRASES

Pretest: Phrases **127**
Verbal Phrases **128**
Prepositional & Appositive Phrases **129**
Absolute Phrases **130**
Effective Phrases **131**
Review: Phrases 132

CLAUSES

Pretest: Clauses **133**
Independent & Dependent Clauses **134**
Adverb, Adjective, & Noun Clauses **135**
Review: Clauses 136

SENTENCE VARIETY

Pretest: Sentences **137**
Kinds of Sentences **138**
Types of Sentences 1 and 2 **139**
Modeling a Sentence 1 and 2 **141**
Review: Sentences 143

SUBJECT-VERB AGREEMENT

Pretest: Subject-Verb Agreement **144**
Subject-Verb Agreement 1, 2, and 3 **145**
Review: Subject-Verb Agreement 148

PRONOUN-ANTECEDENT AGREEMENT

Pretest: Pronoun-Antecedent Agreement **149**
Pronoun-Antecedent Agreement 1 and 2 **150**
Review: Pronoun-Antecedent Agreement 152

Sentence Combining

Pretest: Sentence Combining **153**
Sentence Combining 1 and 2 **154**
Review: Sentence Combining 157

Sentence Problems

SENTENCE FRAGMENTS, COMMA SPLICES, RUN-ONS, & RAMBLING SENTENCES

Pretest: Sentence Problems **159**
Sentence Fragments 1, 2, and 3 **161**
Comma Splices **164**
Run-On Sentences **165**
Rambling Sentences **166**
Review: Sentence Problems 1 167

MISPLACED & DANGLING MODIFIERS

Misplaced Modifiers **168**
Dangling Modifiers **169**

WORDINESS & UNPARALLEL CONSTRUCTION

Wordiness & Deadwood **170**
Unparallel Construction 1 and 2 **171**
Review: Sentence Problems 2 173

SHIFTS IN CONSTRUCTION

Pretest: Shifts in Construction **175**
Shifts in Verb Tense 1 and 2 **176**
Pronoun Shifts 1 and 2 **178**
Shifts in Verb & Pronoun Construction **180**
Review: Shifts in Construction 181

Sentence Review 183

Proofreading Activities

The activities in this section of your *SkillsBook* include sentences that need to be checked for punctuation, mechanics, or correct word choices. Most of the activities also include helpful textbook references. In addition, the **Extend** activities provide follow-up practice of certain skills.

Marking Punctuation   **3**

Editing for Mechanics   **39**

Using the Right Word   **61**

Proofreading Review   **69**

Pretest: Punctuation

> **Place** periods, commas, and apostrophes where they are needed in the following paragraphs.

1   If you're a tourist heading to southern California youre probably on

2   your way to an amusement or theme park But dont overlook a third

3   possibility: Mission San Juan Capistrano It is part of a chain of historic

4   missions—21 in all—that stretches from San Diego to San Francisco

5   For some people the missions represent the high point of Spanish

6   civilization in North America For others, they serve as a painful reminder

7   of the days when Spaniards forced thousands of Native Americans to build

8   these missions work in the fields and change their religious beliefs Today,

9   the missions have become one of Californias main tourist attractions and

10   they are an important link to Californias multicultural past

> **Place** commas, quotation marks, and underlining (for italic) in the following paragraph.

1   Kevin Starr, the state librarian of California talked about the Spanish

2   missions in an interview with the New York Times. He said The missions

3   do have a spell—a hold—over California. And today, as we become

4   increasingly a Latin or a Spanish nation again—Hispanics will soon be the

5   country's largest minority—we begin to appreciate Spanish history as part

6   of United States history. Starr went on to say that California like the rest

7   of the Southwest would not be the same without the historic missions.

Place colons, hyphens, and dashes where they are needed in the following paragraph.

1   California's most famous mission, San Juan Capistrano, is crumbling.

2   Six-inch cracks weaken a sagging dome, and swallows have constructed

3   nests in crevices. Recently the Great Stone Church, which was erected in

4   1806, had a budget for renovation that would have set its builders' heads

5   spinning $10 million! With that kind of money, you might imagine that

6   the 200 year old church could be fully restored to its original glory. The

7   goal, however, is much simpler to keep the mission's walls and roofs from

8   falling down on someone's head. (That actually happened once. Just six

9   years after the Great Stone Church was finished, an earthquake collapsed

10   the roof, killing all 40 worshippers inside.)

Add colons, periods, and commas where they are needed in the following paragraph.

1   Mission San Juan Capistrano is open to the public from 8:30 a m

2   to 500 p m daily For more information write to the following address

3   P O Box 697 San Juan Capistrano CA 92693

Put a Q in the blank if the title should be punctuated with quotation marks; put an I in the blank if the title should be italicized (underlined).

___I___ **1.** Time (magazine)

_____ **2.** New York Times (newspaper)

_____ **3.** The Star-Spangled Banner (song)

_____ **4.** The Road Not Taken (poem)

_____ **5.** World Book (encyclopedia)

_____ **6.** Queen Elizabeth II (ship)

_____ **7.** ESPNNET SportsZone (electronic file)

_____ **8.** 60 Minutes (TV program)

_____ **9.** From Trash to Treasures (magazine article)

End Punctuation

Turn to sections 605.1, 605.4, and 606.1 in *Write Source* for information and examples of end punctuation.

> **Place** periods, question marks, and exclamation points where they are needed in the following narrative. Also put in the necessary capital letters.

1   *A* a small Japanese restaurant recently opened in our town. "let's go "

2   exclaimed my friend John he and I both like trying new things, so this

3   was the perfect place for our next meal out John wondered what kind of

4   tables would be used would they be those low, low tables would we be

5   expected to sit on the floor

6   "I think people kneel and sit on the backs of their legs," I said

7   "that could get very tiring," John replied, "but let's go anyway "

8   we ordered sushi (it was later that I found out sushi is cold rice

9   garnished with raw fish), Hakusai soup, tempura, and, for dessert, some

10   Okinawan sweet fritters

11   "do you know how to use these " John asked, holding up a pair of

12   chopsticks "how are we going to eat soup without a spoon "

13   "I'll show you," I offered I demonstrated by picking up my bowl and

14   slurping the soup

15   "no way," John said. "you can't make that much noise "

16   I replied, "it is one of the few noises that you are allowed to make at

17   a Japanese dining table "

18   we followed the Japanese customs reasonably well the food was

19   beautifully served I declared it "a fine culinary adventure "

Extend: Write three to five sentences, each one making a statement about a different type of food. Then rewrite each of these sentences twice. First, turn each statement into a question; then turn each statement into an exclamation.

Review: End Punctuation

Add end punctuation and capital letters where they are needed below.

1   My friend Tri was explaining to me that origami is the Oriental art

2   of folding paper to make shapes. What kinds of things can you make with

3   origami" I asked

4   "the most popular shapes represent birds, fish, and insects," he

5   answered "more than 1,000 designs are known to exist the possibilities are

6   endless some origami designs have movable parts that imitate the action

7   of the creature or object for example, you can make a crane whose wings

8   flap when you pull the tail"

9   "what materials does origami require" I questioned

10   Tri responded, "all you need are paper and your imagination you can

11   find special origami paper in hobby stores and specialty shops, but almost

12   any paper will work some people even use aluminum foil or tissue paper"

13   "can you cut the paper" I asked

14   "that's actually a topic of debate," he acknowledged "some modern

15   designs do require scissors in contrast, traditional origami forbids the

16   artist to cut, paste, or decorate the paper; only folding is allowed"

17   I then asked him, "who created origami"

18   "the Chinese invented it," he said, "though the Japanese perfected the

19   art, and it has now spread throughout the world origami was originally

20   used in religious ceremonies the Moors introduced origami to Spain, where

21   paper-folding artists made decorative playthings today, origami is popular

22   throughout the world among artists, teachers, and students"

Commas Between Independent Clauses

To form a compound sentence, insert a comma followed by a coordinating conjunction (*and, but, or, nor, for, yet, so*) between the two independent clauses. Turn to 608.1 in *Write Source*. Also turn to page 748 for information about compound sentences.

> **Create** five new compound sentences by combining information from the sentences listed below. Use a comma and a coordinating conjunction between the independent clauses. Use *and, but,* and *so* at least once. You may edit the original sentences as needed.

Medieval knights were trained to fight on horseback.
They could also fight hand to hand.
Overlords gave knights land for their services.
Some knights retired as wealthy men.
Knights were famous for using swords and shields.
They also wielded maces, lances, and battle-axes.
Some knights were crusaders.
They devoted their lives to religious quests.
Medieval knights did not carry guns.
Knighthood continues today.
Knighthood no longer represents just a military role.

1. *Medieval knights were trained to fight on horseback, but they could also fight hand to hand.*

2. _____

    _____

3. _____

    _____

4. _____

    _____

5. _____

    _____

6. _____

    _____

Commas in a Series & to Separate Equal Adjectives

The following examples show how to use commas to separate words and phrases in a series and how to use commas to separate equal adjectives. Turn to 608.2 and 610.2 in *Write Source*.

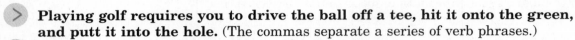 **Playing golf requires you to drive the ball off a tee, hit it onto the green, and putt it into the hole.** (The commas separate a series of verb phrases.)

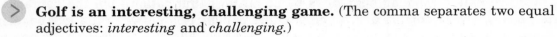 **Golf is an interesting, challenging game.** (The comma separates two equal adjectives: *interesting* and *challenging*.)

Insert commas where they are needed.

1. Golf courses have many different hazards, including trees, roughs, water, and sand traps.

2. The world's most famous and most difficult courses are Saint Andrews in Scotland Augusta National in Georgia and Pebble Beach in California.

3. Prestigious tournaments take place at these beautiful challenging courses.

4. The top four tournaments in men's golf are the PGA the Masters the U.S. Open and the British Open.

5. The top four women's events are the duMaurier Classic in Canada the U.S. Women's Open the LPGA and the Dinah Shore Tournament.

6. Talented experienced golfers can drive a ball more than 250 yards reach the green in two strokes and finish the hole with a single putt.

7. Five of the most notable male golfers of the past century are Bobby Jones Ben Hogan Arnold Palmer Jack Nicklaus and Tiger Woods.

8. "Babe" Didrikson-Zaharias Nancy Lopez Pat Bradley and Amy Alcott are some of the most gifted successful female golfers of the past century.

9. To be a champion golfer, you need to spend years perfecting your drives your chip shots your putting and your patience.

Extend: Write four sentences about a sport or game. In two sentences, use words or phrases in a series. In the other two, include equal adjectives. Use commas correctly.

Commas After Introductory Phrases & Clauses

A comma is used to separate an introductory phrase or clause from the rest of the sentence; it is also used to set off items in a date. Turn to 610.3 and 614.1 in *Write Source* for examples. Then read the examples below carefully. Most readers can tell when the introductory material ends and the main clause begins, but it's still a good idea to learn to distinguish phrases and clauses. (The information about phrases and clauses is on pages 742 and 744 in *Write Source*.)

> *Perhaps best known for his theory describing pressure within a fluid,* **the great mathematician Blaise Pascal was born on June 19, 1623, in France.** (The first comma sets off the introductory phrase, which is a participial phrase modifying "Pascal." Also note how commas set off the date.)

> *Before he was 12 years old,* **Blaise Pascal had mastered the works of earlier mathematicians.** (The comma sets off the introductory adverb clause.)

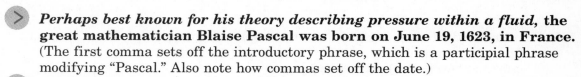

Insert commas where they are needed in the sentences below.

1. When he was only 24 years old , Pascal developed serious health problems and moved to Paris.

2. While living in Paris he became interested in probability theory.

3. After experimenting with probability in many different ways he developed Pascal's triangle.

4. In Pascal's triangle the rows of numbers are designed so that each number is the sum of the two numbers above it.

5. Continuing his work in the field of physics Pascal produced the principle called Pascal's Law.

6. Often used to help design and develop new devices Pascal's Law led to the invention of hydraulic jacks and air brakes.

7. Although many of his peers doubted that a vacuum could exist Pascal helped prove that air has weight and its absence can produce a vacuum.

8. Following a severe bout with depression Pascal had a religious experience on November 23 1654 that changed his life.

9. After Pascal entered a monastery in January 1655 he became a monk.

   Writers INC 490.4, 491.1, 492.1, and pp. 552–553

10. From 1658 until his death Pascal lived at the monastery and worked on many projects.

11. By writing a defense of the Christian faith Pascal became famous in yet another way.

12. After he died fragments of his uncompleted manuscript were found and published in a work titled *Pensées*.

13. Writing about his theory that there is a limit to what a human can understand Pascal established himself as a philosopher and theologian.

14. Still considered one of the greatest mathematicians and philosophers of all time Pascal died on August 19 1662 at the age of 39.

Fill in the following blanks. Turn to 458.4 and 459.1 in *Write Source.*

1. Introductory phrases are often prepositional phrases or _____ phrases.

2. When a prepositional phrase follows the independent clause, the _____ is often omitted.

3. You may also omit the _____ if the introductory phrase is _____ .

4. When an adverb clause _____ the main clause and begins with *although, even though, while,* or another conjunction expressing a _____ , a comma is used.

5. A comma is not used if the adverb clause following the main clause is needed to _____ .

Extend: Write five sentences about someone you know. Begin each of your sentences with an introductory phrase or clause. Include dates using commas in at least two of your sentences.

Review: Commas 1

> **Insert commas where they are needed.**

1. When it was launched in 1958, the *Edmund Fitzgerald* was the largest strongest ore ship on the Great Lakes.

2. Neither its strength its size nor its experienced captain could prevent the *Edmund Fitzgerald* from sinking on November 10 1975 in Lake Superior.

3. Loaded with 26,000 tons of iron ore pellets the *Edmund Fitzgerald* sailed from Superior, Wisconsin, on November 10 1975.

4. The sunny November day looked calm but a storm with strong blustery winds and waves in excess of 15 feet lay ahead.

5. As the storm gained strength Captain Ernest McSorley bore north across Lake Superior.

6. Seeking the shelter of the Canadian shore and Whitefish Bay the capable quick-thinking captain continued to bear north.

7. But luck was not with the captain the crew or the ship for both the radar system and its backup failed.

8. Not only did the ship's radar system fail but the storm also took out the electrical power to Whitefish Point's light and radio beacon.

9. The light came back on but the radio beacon did not.

10. Captain McSorley's final brief message at 7:10 p.m. was "We're holding our own."

11. Gordon Lightfoot's song "The Wreck of the *Edmund Fitzgerald*" tells the tale of the ship the storm and the tragedy.

Commas to Set Off Contrasted Elements & Appositives

Commas are used to set off appositives, explanatory words, and items in an address. Turn to 610.1, 612.1, and 614.2 in *Write Source* for additional information.

Insert commas where they are needed below.

1. Our teacher, Mr. Goodman, assigned a project on volcanoes.

2. My cousin a freshman in college has seen a volcano.

3. I sent a letter to him at 889 West Dayton Street Madison Wisconsin 54421 to ask for some information about volcanoes.

4. I knew that my cousin a very observant person would have good facts.

5. My cousin sent a letter back to me at 39924 Raven Drive Lake Villa Illinois 60046.

6. He wrote me that he had seen Mauna Loa a volcano in Hawaii.

7. A volcano can spew magma hot molten rock hundreds of feet into the air.

8. The least violent type of eruption a Hawaiian eruption is characterized by very fluid lava and an occasional lava fountain.

9. The most violent eruption a Peleean eruption includes a violent ejection of volcanic ash.

10. Stromboli an active volcano off the coast of Italy erupts constantly.

11. My cousin an avid photographer sent me some photographs of volcanoes.

12. He also gave me the name of a volcanologist he knows who lives at 32454 Oak Drive Los Angeles California 90025.

Extend: Write three to five sentences about a tourist attraction you'd like to visit. Include an appositive or explanatory words in each sentence, using commas to set them off correctly.

Other Uses of Commas

Use commas to set off dialogue, nouns of direct address, and interjections. Turn to 616.1, 616.2, and 616.4 in *Write Source* for examples.

Insert commas where they are needed below.

1. "Today," our science teacher said, "we are going to learn about thunderclouds."

2. "Mrs. Stellflag how high can a thundercloud rise?" Henry asked.

3. "They can reach up to 50,000 feet," Sally said.

4. "Thunderclouds are formed when warm, moist air rises toward cooler air" Mrs. Stellflag added.

5. "Mrs. Stellflag is that when the water condenses?" Kristy wondered.

6. "That's right. When the warm, moist air hits the cold air Kristy the water and dust particles create raindrops" answered Mrs. Stellflag.

7. "The clouds that are formed" Mrs. Stellflag continued "are called cumulonimbus clouds."

8. "So Mrs. Stellflag are those the huge, towerlike clouds?" Jaleel asked.

9. "My goodness you students really know a lot about this" she said.

10. "These clouds commonly produce large gusts of wind" Mrs. Stellflag continued "and can also produce tornadoes."

11. "Yeah I remember the thunderstorm on July 4, 2004, because it took out three of our huge oak trees" Laura added.

12. "Don't forget that thunderstorms are always accompanied by lightning" Mrs. Stellflag warned "which adds to their destructive power."

Extend: Write a conversation between two people discussing recent weather. Use commas to set off dialogue, nouns of direct address, and interjections. (See pages 324–325 in *Write Source* for a sample dialogue.)

Commas with Nonrestrictive Phrases & Clauses 1

Nonrestrictive phrases and clauses *are not* essential to the meaning of the sentence. Restrictive phrases and clauses *are* essential. Study the examples below. Turn to 612.2 in *Write Source* for further information.

> Ferdinand Magellan, *whose Spanish name is Fernão de Magalhães,* was the leader of the first expedition around the world. (nonrestrictive clause)

> The sailor *who actually completed the expedition* was Juan Sebastián del Cano. (restrictive clause)

Label each sentence below. Write **R** if it contains a restrictive phrase or clause, or **N** if it contains a nonrestrictive phrase or clause. Insert commas to set off the nonrestrictive phrases and clauses.

N **1.** The voyage, which was originally planned to find a new trade route to the East, left Spain on September 20, 1519.

_____ **2.** Magellan who was an experienced Portuguese sailor took with him 240 men on five ships.

_____ **3.** The strait at the tip of South America that Magellan sailed through was later named for him.

_____ **4.** Ahead lay the vast Pacific Ocean which Magellan himself named.

_____ **5.** The *Santiago* which was one of the ships on the voyage accidentally beached itself on a sandbar.

_____ **6.** Magellan sailed his remaining ships to a group of islands located in the Philippines.

_____ **7.** Magellan who became involved in a local war was killed on April 27, 1521, on Mactan Island.

_____ **8.** The *Victoria* which was the only ship to finish the voyage returned to Spain on September 6, 1522.

_____ **9.** This journey disproved the theory that the world was flat.

Commas with Nonrestrictive Phrases & Clauses 2

Nonrestrictive phrases and clauses (sometimes called nonessential word groups) can be removed from a sentence without changing its basic meaning. Always use commas to set off nonrestrictive phrases and clauses. Turn to 612.2 in *Write Source* and study the examples.

> **Insert** commas in the sentences below to set off nonrestrictive phrases and clauses. (Not all sentences need commas.)

1. Programs of the American Red Cross, which are funded by contributions, aim to prevent suffering among all people in time of war or peace.

2. In 1864, Jean Henri Dunant founded an organization of volunteers to aid any person regardless of nationality wounded in war.

3. The Red Cross which grew from Dunant's organization now has societies in more than 135 countries.

4. Aid to disaster victims which is provided free of charge includes food, clothing, medical service, and shelter.

5. Families separated by war, disasters, or other emergencies are often reunited by Red Cross societies throughout the world.

6. Its national transplant service begun in 1984 provides bone, skin, and organs to doctors and their patients.

7. The Red Cross volunteers who serve in military medical facilities provide assistance to members of the armed forces.

8. Many safety programs including the familiar first aid, swimming, and babysitting courses are offered by local Red Cross chapters.

9. Red Cross youth activities which are designed to develop leadership skills range from volunteer hospital service to international friendship projects.

Extend: Write four sentences about a natural disaster (earthquake, tornado, hurricane, and so on). Two of the sentences should contain a nonrestrictive clause; the other two should include a restrictive clause. Use commas where necessary.

Review: Commas 2

Insert commas where they are needed in the sentences below.

1   The concept of "breaching the peace," known today as "disorderly

2   conduct" has its roots in England. It dates back to a time when the

3   monarch who was believed to be the supreme ruler proclaimed a royal

4   right to peace. Whenever someone committed a crime against the royal

5   laws the offender was arrested for disturbing "the king's peace."

6   Today the term "breach of peace" is seldom used. However, on October

7   30 2005 at about 1:00 a.m. my father and I came to understand the

8   meaning of this phrase when the doorbell woke us.

9   A voice outside said "Mr. Hurley I need to speak to you and your son

10   Reginald." My father opened the door to find two plainclothes police officers.

11   "What's the problem?" my father asked.

12   "According to our reports you and your son were disturbing the peace

13   up until about 30 minutes ago" one police officer said.

14   "Well" Father began "what did we supposedly do?"

15   The police officer replied "We understand that you and your son have

16   a plastic clown's head which you obtained from the St. Bartholomew's fund-

17   raiser and that you put the clown's head on the end of a pole. You then

18   took it to the home of Nelson Giles on 143 Surf Street held it up to his

19   window and made loud laughing noises until you woke him."

20   About this time Mr. Giles appeared from behind a tree laughing

21   uncontrollably. "I'd like you to meet my cousins John and Karl. We really

22   had you didn't we?"

Semicolons to Join Independent Clauses

Semicolons may be used to connect closely related sentences or independent clauses, sometimes with conjunctive adverbs. For examples and a list of conjunctive adverbs, turn to 618.2 in *Write Source*.

> **Join** the following pairs of sentences using either a semicolon alone or a semicolon with a conjunctive adverb.

1. Brazil is a vast country. It is almost as big as the United States.

2. Spanish is spoken throughout much of South America. The official language of Brazil is Portuguese.

3. Brazil is the largest country in South America. It occupies almost half the continent.

4. Brazil is a populous country. It has more inhabitants than all the other South American countries combined.

5. The Amazon, the earth's largest river, flows through Brazil. It carries more water than any other river.

6. One of Brazil's greatest resources is the rain forest. It is quickly disappearing.

7. Regional clothing styles are distinctive. For example, women in the state of Bahia wear colorful skirts, bright blouses, and many bracelets.

8. Brazil has more than 6,000 miles of coastline. Thousands of people go to the beaches to swim, fish, and boat.

9. Soccer is the favorite sport. One Brazilian soccer star, Pele, became known as the world's greatest soccer player.

10. There is an average of one car for every 15 people. Most Brazilians travel by bus.

Extend: Write six to eight very short sentences about the city or state in which you live. Exchange papers with a classmate. Combine one another's sentences using semicolons.

   Writers INC 494.1

Semicolons to Separate Word Groups Containing Commas

Semicolons separate groups of words (within a sentence) that already contain commas. The items in each group must be related. Turn to 618.3 in *Write Source* for an example.

> **Write** sentences that include lists of the items below. Use semicolons to punctuate each sentence.

1. *Things found in the woods: animals, plants, rocks*

While in the woods, I saw chipmunks, deer, and rabbits; ferns,

mushrooms, and ivy; quartz, granite, and sandstone rocks.

2. *Favorite foods: fruits, vegetables, cheeses*

_____

_____

_____

3. *Things in your room: books, clothes, shoes*

_____

_____

_____

4. *Places you've been (or want to visit): states, national parks, other countries*

_____

_____

_____

5. *Things to pack for a trip: clothes, personal items, books*

_____

_____

_____

Colons 1

The examples below illustrate how colons are used in the salutation of a business letter, between numbers indicating time, and to emphasize a word or a group of words. Turn to 620.1–620.3 in *Write Source*.

> **Dear Mr. Baker:**
> (The colon follows a salutation in a business letter.)

> **My curfew is 9:30 p.m. on weekdays.**
> (The colon separates the numbers *9* and *30* to indicate time.)

> **We had to find the puzzle's missing piece: the mysterious black one.**
> (The colon is used to emphasize the phrase *the mysterious black one*.)

Insert colons where they are needed in the letter below.

1   Dear Mrs. Klein⁀

2   We are happy to inform you that we have found something of yours a

3   small purse. We know that you left it in our restaurant sometime between

4   800 p.m. and 930 p.m. last Friday.

5   You may come and pick up your purse anytime we are open. Our

6   hours are from 800 a.m. to 945 p.m. on weekdays and from 1000 a.m.

7   to 1000 p.m. on weekends.

8   We will be able to verify your identity by using the picture

9   identification we found in the purse your driver's license.

10   There is just one last issue we need to address the reward. We

11   appreciate a reward being offered, but we won't be able to accept it.

12   Rather, we recommend you do this visit us again in the future.

13   Sincerely,

14   The Red River Inn Staff

Extend: Write three to five sentences about a time you lost something. Use at least one colon in each sentence to indicate time or to emphasize a word or group of words.

Writers INC 494.3–494.5

Colons 2

Colons are used to introduce a list; to distinguish between title and subtitle, volume and page, and chapter and verse in literature; and to introduce a sentence, a question, or a quotation. Turn to 620.4–620.6 in *Write Source*.

Insert colons where they are needed in the sentences below.

---

1. Booker T. Washington focused on three things during his lifetime : education, freedom, and civil rights.

2. He tells his story in his book *Up from Slavery An Autobiography by Booker T. Washington.*

3. Booker T. Washington once made this observation "My experience is that there is something in human nature which always makes an individual recognize and reward merit."

4. Washington held many different jobs salt-furnace laborer, coal miner, house servant, night janitor, and, ultimately, teacher.

5. As a teacher, Washington taught African Americans the subjects that he believed were most important for success writing, reading, and agriculture.

6. He remembers thinking as a child that reading was very important "I recall that I had an intense longing to learn to read. I determined . . . that, if I accomplished nothing else in life, I would in some way get enough education to enable me to read."

7. Washington summed up his belief in the future with these words "In the long run, the world is going to have the best, and any difference in race, religion, or previous history will not long keep the world from what it wants."

Extend: Compose three to five sentences about a book you've read. Use a colon in each sentence to introduce a list or to introduce a sentence, question, or quotation.

Review: Semicolons & Colons

> **Insert** colons and semicolons correctly in the sentences below.

1. I decided to call my grandmother yesterday**;** I hadn't talked to her in a long time.

2. The doctor will not be in until 1000 a.m. tomorrow however, you can go to the clinic if you need immediate care.

3. Ms. Anderson asked one question before class started "Did everyone remember to bring his or her book?"

4. With the party coming up, Christoph made a list of things to do water the lawn, order the cake, and hire a clown.

5. Darcy read aloud the inscription from John 8 32—"The truth will set you free."

6. There is one thing you must remember when hiking that trail stay away from poison ivy.

7. The storm became impossible to ignore thunderclouds darkened the sky, lightning flashed, and thunder rumbled.

8. At our supermarket you will find detergent, scrub brushes, and toilet-bowl cleaners in aisle 6 bread, peanut butter, and jelly in aisle 11 and soup, crackers, and seasonings in aisle 15.

9. Our heroine was stuck in the abandoned warehouse meanwhile, her trusty sidekick was stuck in traffic.

10. In class we talked about two things the rights of the homeless and the problems with the Social Security Administration.

Hyphens 1

A hyphen is used to make compound words (*son-in-law, president-elect*), to join the words in compound numbers (*twenty-one, ninety-nine*), to form new words beginning with certain prefixes (*self-made, ex-mayor*), to indicate a span of time (*1902–1982*), and to join two or more words that serve as a single adjective (*up-to-date, cream-filled*). Turn to 624.1, 626.1, 624.2, 626.3, and 624.3 in *Write Source* for more information.

> **Insert** hyphens where they are needed in the sentences below.

1. My great-grandmother has been eighty-one for three minutes and twenty-two seconds.

2. A water repellent tent is a must on any camping trip.

3. Grandpa always admired self made men and women, the pull yourself up by the bootstraps type.

4. During her first term as senator (1993 1999), Ms. Millicent supported campaign finance reform.

5. Is that what is called ready to wear clothing?

6. On Friday, we will have a half hour lunch.

7. Great grandfather likes Stanley's twice baked potatoes.

8. The coach has a change your attitude look on his face.

9. He was a make my day type of teacher.

10. A worm crawled out of the half eaten apple.

11. I think the dates for the Civil War were 1860 1865.

12. Did Liam say his mother in law was a delight?

13. I must remember to use a hyphen in numbers twenty one to ninety nine.

14. The soon to be father fainted.

15. Small minded people will dislike the change.

Hyphens 2

A hyphen is used to join a letter to a word, to join the elements of a written-out fraction, and to join the numbers in a vote or a score. A hyphen is also used when two or more words share a common element that appears only with the last term. Turn to 624.4, 626.1, and 626.3 in *Write Source*.

> **Insert** hyphens where they are needed in the following sentences.

1. It was a hot day, and my T-shirt was sticking to my back.

2. Work on the deck was about two thirds done.

3. Our radio was tuned to a ball game; the Sox were up 2 0.

4. The house we were working on was an A frame from the late '70s.

5. It belonged to Jack's mother, who was always taking pre and post repair photographs.

6. We were using three and four inch nails.

7. The screws we used were three fourths of an inch long.

8. I asked the guys if they wanted to change to the Cubs game, and the vote was 4 1 in favor.

9. As I was getting up to change the station, Jerry asked me to get him the five, seven, and nine sixteenths wrenches.

10. That is when I discovered that one third of the tools were missing.

11. Before long, we watched as the police car made a U turn and pulled up.

12. Then Jack's four year old son appeared.

13. "I'm building a T house," he said proudly. (He meant "tree house.")

14. We laughed and then voted 5 0 not to have him arrested for taking our tools.

Extend: Write four sentences about building something. In two of the sentences, use a hyphen to join two or more words that serve as a single adjective. In the other two sentences, use a hyphen to join words sharing a common element that appears only with the last term.

Dashes

Dashes are used to indicate a sudden break or change in a sentence, to set off an introductory series, to set off parenthetical material, to show interrupted speech, and to emphasize a word or word group at the end of a sentence. Turn to 640.1–640.5 in *Write Source*.

Write the number of the rule in *Write Source* that explains why a dash is used in each example below.

**640.1 (or)
640.3**

1. I really like my room—bright, clean, and cheerful—after I painted it.

2. Discipline, honesty, love—these are what the world needs.

3. I—must reach—the control box—before it is too late.

4. It was 1945—the year World War II ended—when Jimmy finally came home.

5. The unique chime made the clock a piece of furniture that people would have loved—to throw out a window.

6. A cup of flour, a teaspoon of baking soda, a pinch of salt—all I needed to make the paste was right here.

7. It was Mr. Peabody—the elderly man who lives on Lilac Road—who donated the rare book to the library.

8. I—can't—breathe—because—the aliens are turning off the oxygen mixer.

9. We heard the noise—clank, ding, bong—and I knew that it would be a long time before the car would be zip-zap-zooming anywhere.

10. With two whole dollars in my pocket, I was really rolling—right down Poorman's Alley.

Write two sentences of your own that use dashes to set off an introductory series in a sentence.

_____

_____

_____

_____

Review: Hyphens & Dashes

> **Insert** hyphens or dashes where they are needed in the sentences below.

1. My brother-in-law is very friendly.

2. I don't think a U turn would be wise here.

3. Four, six, and eight foot boards those are the only oak boards we have in stock.

4. This half eaten pear is the worst thing I've ever seen in your sock drawer.

5. Two thirds of the people in the audience think that the score should have been 4 3.

6. Sometimes I can be a scaredy cat person.

7. Some things in the room the lamp, the desk, the couch simply do not match anything.

8. The bug eyed young man alone and terrified screamed at the bear.

9. My great great grandmother made banana bread truly scrumptious banana bread.

10. The senate vote yesterday was 54 46 for the new tax bill.

11. I'm not sure that mid January is the best time for a swimming party.

12. My sister is a pro at what she does best writing free verse poetry.

13. Grease, mud, dust, and dirt what would a garage be without them?

14. Only one fourth of the votes supported our ex mayor.

15. Her self centered attitude is not appealing to most people.

16. The bell like shape of the house made it an oddity.

17. Yes well, no well, maybe well, I don't know.

18. My sixteen year old sister likes to drive drive a convertible, that is.

Apostrophes to Form Possessives 1

The possessive form of a noun shows ownership. Ownership can be singular (*Joe's book*) or plural (*teachers' cars*). Turn to 628.2–628.3 in *Write Source* for more information.

> **Add** an apostrophe and, when needed, an *s* to any noun that should be possessive.

1. One of Cleveland's biggest attractions is the Rock and Roll Hall of Fame, a fantastic showcase for musicians and their achievements.

2. The Hall of Fames founders were leaders in the music business. They created the museum to recognize the industrys most important contributors.

3. Elvis Presley, Buddy Holly, Chuck Berry, and Ray Charles were four of the Halls first inductees.

4. One exhibit features Elvis Presley. It includes Elvis report card, his army uniform, and one of his guitars.

5. Presleys epithet, "The King of Rock and Roll," fits Mississippis best-known rocker. Many of the Kings songs topped the charts; in fact, he recorded more Top 40 hits (107) and more Top 10 hits (38) than any other artist.

6. Each year, the Rock and Roll Hall of Fame Foundations nominating committee reviews hundreds of performers careers.

7. Many nominees music could be considered gospel, blues, or country as well as rock and roll.

8. Each years ballots go to about 1,000 of the worlds experts on rock and roll.

9. The experts votes determine who gets into the Hall of Fame.

10. An inductees fame must stand the test of time, because an artists eligibility doesn't begin until 25 years after his or her first record is released.

Extend: Write three to five sentences about someone you think should be in the Rock and Roll Hall of Fame. Use at least three nouns that show possession. Check your sentences for the correct use of apostrophes.

Apostrophes to Form Possessives 2

Possession can be shared by more than one noun. Turn to 628.4 in *Write Source.*

> **Add** an apostrophe, or an apostrophe and **s,** where needed.

1. The Marx Brothers were one of the funniest groups to act in vaudeville's palaces, Hollywood's films, and Broadway's theaters.

2. Groucho, Harpo, and Chico real names were Julius, Arthur, and Leonard.

3. Two other brothers, Milton and Herbert, appeared in the act from time to time. Milton and Herbert stage names were Gummo and Zeppo.

4. The Marx Brothers made 12 films, but producers and directors didn't fully know how to use Harpo, Groucho, and Chico talents.

5. Often the brothers zaniness was bogged down by bad songs and boring subplots. Only *Animal Crackers, Duck Soup,* and *Horsefeathers* gave the brothers full freedom to go wild.

6. Music played a part in the brothers films. In *Animal Crackers,* Groucho, Chico, and Harpo opening musical number showed their combined talents. Groucho sang while Chico played the piano and Harpo played the harp.

7. Hungerdunger, Hungerdunger, Hungerdunger, and McCormack law office is one of the settings in *Animal Crackers.*

8. Some comedy teams are famous for one special routine. Examples include Abbott and Costello "Who's on First," Martin and Lewis "Crazy Conductor," and Rowan and Martin "I Didn't Know That."

9. But every one of the Marx Brothers films is filled with Groucho, Harpo, and Chico own unique gags.

Extend: Think of objects or activities that you and several of your friends share. Write sentences describing these objects or activities. Use the correct possessive forms of your names.

Apostrophes to Form Possessives 3

To show the possessive form of a compound noun, place the possessive ending after the last word. Turn to 630.2 in *Write Source* for information and examples.

Underline the correct choice in each italicized pair below.

1. My (<u>sister-in-law's</u>, *sister's-in-laws*) dream was really weird.

2. In it, she was the president of the United States, and I was the (*speaker of the House of Representatives'*, *speaker's of the House of Representatives*) dog walker.

3. Our new president, my sister-in-law, began changing the government according to Article II, Section 3 of the Constitution. The (*commander in chief's*, *commander's in chiefs*) plan started with adjourning Congress.

4. She told the senators and representatives not to come back until they agreed on a budget. Her (*plan of attack's*, *plan's of attack*) direction then switched to international matters.

5. My sister-in-law appointed my (*brother's-in-laws*, *brother-in-law's*) uncle as secretary of state. The new (*secretary of state's*, *secretary's of states*) first duty was to issue free passports to every United States citizen.

6. Then the three of us gave a party for the secretary-general of the United Nations and the (*secretary-general's*, *secretary-generals'*) family.

7. The fun really started when the soup was served. The (*aide-de-camp's*, *aide's-de-camp*) hands were shaking so badly that he spilled a bowl of soup in his lap.

8. Finally my (*sister's-in-laws*, *sister-in-law's*) alarm clock rang, and she escaped from this political nightmare.

Extend: Write three to five sentences about a dream or daydream. Use correct possessive endings on at least three compound nouns.

Other Uses for Apostrophes

Apostrophes show where letters or numbers have been left out. They are also used to form plurals and contractions. Turn to 628.1 and 630.4 in *Write Source*.

> **Add** apostrophes where they are needed.

1. Some clocks dont have 1s, 2s, or 3s on their faces; only lines indicate where those numbers would be.

2. Ive even seen watches that dont have anything but the hands on their faces.

3. "Bye, Mom! Were goin swimmin!" Alf shouted as he and Ralph ran out the door.

4. I cant believe its been 10 years since I graduated in 95.

5. Ramundo's four Cs and two Ds on his report card wont make his father very happy.

6. The instructions for the bread machine list many *dos* and *donts*.

7. Theyre recycling many of the fashions from the 60s and 70s.

8. Kids are even movin and groovin to songs from that era.

9. Stir n Serve Vegetables are my favorite.

10. My curfew used to be ten oclock, but now its later.

11. It isnt unusual to hear public speakers use a lot of *uhs* and *ums*.

12. Doreen mistakenly used %s in her paper when she should have spelled out *percent*.

13. Angie waved at Greg and said, "Gnight!"

14. The forty-niners enjoyed ridin and ropin when they werent prospectin for gold.

Extend: Write three to five sentences analyzing your ideal report card. Use apostrophes in your writing to form contractions and the plural forms of letters or numbers.

Review: Apostrophes

> **Add** an apostrophe and, when it is needed, an *s* to each noun or pronoun that should be possessive. Also insert apostrophes in other places where needed.

1   In 1848, James Marshall discovered gold at John Sutters sawmill. The

2   next year, 50,000 people headed to Californias goldfields. The luckiest

3   prospectors dreams came true: they found gold. Other people became rich

4   by selling supplies to the areas many miners.

5   In a few months, 75 percent of San Franciscos men had left their

6   homes, giving in to the goldfields allure. When the news of gold reached

7   the East Coast in 49, many easterners also headed west. But it was at

8   least three months journey to California. Ships had to sail around South

9   America or stop at Panama, where men trekked across Panamas isthmus

10   to catch a second ship on the other side. Other forty-niners traveled by

11   land, crossing Nebraskas plains and Colorados mountains. Everyones

12   wagons started rolling before six oclock and didnt stop until dark.

13   Gold fever spread to Colorados, Nevadas, and Montanas rivers and

14   mountains. In 1859 in Nevada, Henry Comstock and his partners put their

15   Xs on the claim that produced the Comstock Lode, one of the United States

16   richest silver mines. At first, the Comstock Lodes miners threw away the

17   black rock mixed in with the gold, not knowing that theyd found pure silver.

18   Soon, a silver fever overtook miners, and they flocked to the Comstock Lode.

19   Virginia City, Nevada, one of Nevadas most colorful mining towns, sprang up.

20   Today, Virginia Citys opera house, saloons, steam locomotive, old

21   houses, and boardwalks keep its history alive. Tourists enjoy the citys old-

22   time atmosphere.

Quotation Marks with Dialogue

Quotation marks are used to set off dialogue from the rest of a sentence. Turn to 632.1 and 632.2 in *Write Source* for more information and examples. Commas are used to set off a speaker's exact words. Turn to 616.1 in *Write Source*.

> **Add** quotation marks and commas where they are needed.

1   Ms. Quing says " Quasars are the most luminous objects in the universe.

2   The brightest known quasar has a luminosity 30,000 times that of the Milky

3   Way. " She continues Picture all the stars in our galaxy outshined by one

4   quasar.

5   As he listens to the physics teacher, Bill whispers to Sarah I love

6   astronomy.

7   Sarah replies I do too, but I have trouble imagining the vastness of

8   space.

9   Ms. Quing continues Now imagine the darkest spot in the sky; telescopes

10   show even these spaces are full of galaxies full of stars.

11   Ms. Quing, Bill asks is star travel a possibility?

12   Theoretically, yes answers Ms. Quing. However, no one has any idea how

13   to make such travel possible.

14   Sarah says I read that surpassing the speed of light will mean strange

15   space-time interaction. What does that mean?

16   No one is sure, Sarah," Ms. Quing states. Some think such speeds will

17   warp space itself. Think about this! The traveller will not age as rapidly as

18   the people who send astronauts to the stars.

Extend: Write a short conversation between two or more friends about a favorite television show. Punctuate the dialogue correctly.

Writers INC 501.1, 500.3, 492.3, and p. 159

Quotation Marks with Direct Quotations

Quotation marks are placed before and after direct quotations. They also set off words that are being used in a special way. Turn to 632.1 and page 634.2 in *Write Source*.

> **Put** quotation marks around direct quotations and words used in special ways.

1   Mr. Oquendo, my social studies teacher, said, "Presidents and other

2   politicians are good sources of quotations." He told us that Calvin Coolidge,

3   who was given the nickname Silent Cal, was his favorite politician.

4   I asked, How can a person known as Silent Cal be quotable?

5   Why don't you find out? Mr. Oquendo asked in return.

6   So I did. Silent Cal's slogan was "Keep Cool with Coolidge." Ironically,

7   the word uncool came to mind when I considered Coolidge, who was a

8   sour-faced man. A reporter once wrote, It looks like he is always sucking

9   on lemons.

10   Coolidge thought that government should leave business alone and not

11   spend money helping people. The chief business of the American people is

12   business, he stated. Describing America in the 1920s, he said, Civilization

13   and profits go hand in hand. When he left office, he commented, Perhaps

14   one of the most important accomplishments of my administration has been

15   minding my own business. Although some people benefited from this

16   so-called Coolidge Prosperity, many others would not have called it

17   prosperity. Some of Coolidge's policies led to the Great Depression.

18   I guess Mr. Oquendo was right; the nickname Silent Cal was ironic.

19   One history book concluded, Cal really wasn't silent: He gave more

20   speeches than any of the 29 presidents before him!

Extend: Does a friend of yours have a favorite saying? ("That's the way it goes," "Later, dude," and so on) Write a short dialogue between you and your friend containing one of these sayings.

Double & Single Quotation Marks

Single quotation marks are used to punctuate a quotation within another quotation. Turn to 634.1 in *Write Source* for an explanation and example.

> **Add** single and double quotation marks where they are needed.

1   My English teacher, Mr. Gobel, said, "The first time that the term

2   'football player' appeared in print was in Shakespeare's *King Lear,* when

3   Kent insults Oswald, saying, 'you base [lowlife] football player.'"

4   Mr. Gobel explained, It's important to understand that in England,

5   football is the term for soccer, so Kent is actually calling Oswald a lowlife

6   soccer player.

7   But football, even back then, was considered a rough game, Mr.

8   Gobel continued. From 1314 to 1603, it was banned by 10 different kings,

9   including Henry VIII. Imagine Henry VIII saying, No more football or off

10 with your heads! Everyone laughed.

11 Mr. Gobel was just warming up to his subject. He stated, In 1823,

12 William Ellis of Rugby School in England picked up the football [soccer

13 ball] and ran with it. The game of rugby football was invented. With it,

14 rules changed, and a new term came into being: tackle.

15 After a dramatic pause, Mr. Gobel said, Finally, American football

16 developed from rugby. He paused again, smiled, and said, Enough terms.

17 Your assignment for the weekend is to watch the Super Bowl. Class

18 dismissed!

Extend: Write three sentences your teacher might use to explain literary terms to your class. In addition to using his or her own words, imagine that your teacher is quoting directly from *Write Source* pages 314–315 and 322. This means you will have to use double *and* single quotation marks to punctuate your sentences correctly.

Writers INC 501.3 and pp. 253–261

Italics (Underlining) & Quotation Marks 1

Quotation marks or italics (shown by underlining) identify the titles of books, movies, songs, lectures, videos, and other works, as well as the names of ships and aircraft. Turn to 634.3 and 636.1–636.2 in *Write Source* for information and examples.

> **Add** quotation marks or underlining to correctly set off titles and special names in the sentences below.

1. Many people are interested in disasters such as the sinking of the <u>Titanic</u> or the crashing of the <u>Hindenburg</u>.

2. Films about the ill-fated Titanic include Titanica, an IMAX movie; A Night to Remember, a British production; and Titanic, a Hollywood extravaganza.

3. A Night to Remember was based on a book written in 1955 by Walter Lord. In 1985 Lord wrote a sequel, The Night Lives On. The short story Lifeboat, by James W. Herndon, also describes this famous disaster.

4. As the Titanic sank, the band supposedly played Nearer My God to Thee.

5. The American Heritage magazine article Titanic: Not-So-True Romance reports that survivors remember the band's last song being Dream of Autumn.

6. Titanic: A New Musical opened on Broadway in 1997. The play included the song Dressed in Your Pajamas in the Grand Salon.

7. The Discovery of the Titanic, a book written by Robert D. Ballard, provides detailed information about the ship's remains on the seafloor.

8. Explorers have dived the 12,468 feet to the wreck in the manned submersibles the Nautile and the Alvin. A robotic ship, Jason, Jr., has explored inside the wreck.

9. A lecture at the Maritime Museum, entitled Let It Be, strongly recommended an end to all future explorations of the Titanic.

Extend: Write four or five sentences about your favorite films, stories, books, TV shows, or CD's. Use quotation marks or underlining to correctly identify the titles.

Italics (Underlining) & Quotation Marks 2

Quotation marks or italics (shown by underlining) identify the titles of lectures, plays, magazines, CD's, TV shows, and other works. Turn to 634.3 and 636.1–636.2 in *Write Source*.

> **Add** quotation marks or underlining to correctly set off titles.

1. Our history teacher gave a lecture titled "The '60s and '70s: Been There, Done That."

2. In 1966, Star Trek began its run on television. The pilot episode, The Cage, starred only two members of the original cast. NBC wanted a second pilot, so Where No Man Has Gone Before was produced.

3. The top single at the end of 1971 was the theme from the movie Shaft.

4. In one of his book's chapters, titled The Schizophrenic Sixties, pop-culture author Charles Panati wrote, "Hippies in San Francisco . . . began to tie-dye every garment that would absorb color."

5. Go-go boots were also a '60s fashion hit. In an interview with Spin magazine, Madonna said, "Nancy Sinatra was my first pop idol . . . with go-go boots, miniskirt, and fake eyelashes." Sinatra sang These Boots Are Made for Walkin'.

6. Roger McGuinn of the Byrds wore tinted granny glasses on TV's Ed Sullivan Show and on the album cover of Turn! Turn! Turn! Soon after, everyone was wearing granny glasses.

7. In that era, Harper Lee's novel To Kill a Mockingbird won the Pulitzer prize, and the musical A Chorus Line won a prize for drama.

8. The Godfather was the most popular novel of the '70s.

Extend: Write three to five sentences describing popular fads, books, TV shows, and films. Use quotation marks and underlining correctly to identify the titles.

Writers INC 500.1 and 502.1–502.2

Review: Quotation Marks & Italics (Underlining)

Put single quotation marks, double quotation marks, and underlining where needed.

1   The documentary film <u>The Civil War</u> uses diaries and journals to

2   describe this important event in United States history. For instance, after

3   four years of fighting, food was scarce in the Confederacy. All kinds of

4   stories were later told about just how desperate things actually became.

5   In his journal, one soldier wrote, We found no one who will exchange

6   eatables for Confederate money. So we are devouring our clothes.

7   Generals Grant and Lee had been fighting each other in Petersburg,

8   Virginia, for nine months. Lee asked the Confederate Congress for more

9   men and supplies: I have been up to see Congress, and they do not seem

10   able to do anything except eat peanuts and chew tobacco. Lee even asked

11   that slaves be used in the army, and the Confederate Congress agreed.

12   The Richmond Examiner reported: The country will not deny General Lee

13   anything he may ask for.

14   But it was not enough. Soon Federal troops entered Richmond, the

15   Confederacy's capital. One Confederate officer described the chaos in the

16   city as follows: Every now and then, as a magazine [shell] exploded, a

17   column of white smoke rose . . . followed by a deafening sound. The

18   ground seemed to rock and tremble. . . . Hundreds of shells would explode

19   in the air. . . . Then all was still, for the moment, except for the dull

20   roar and crackle of the fast-spreading fires.

21   The Confederates left Richmond, some singing Dixie. Their White

22   House soon became Union headquarters. Walking through the ruined city

23 afterward, a reporter for the New York World wrote, There is no sound of

24 life, but the stillness of a catacomb. . . .

25   Lee's army headed west in search of food. General John B. Gordon

26 said about Lee's retreat, The lines were alternately forming, fighting, and

27 retreating, making one continuous battle. A boy soldier came running by.

28 When asked why he was running, he shouted back, I'm running 'cause I

29 can't fly!

30   Lee stopped at Appomattox Court House where he soon surrendered to

31 Grant with these words: I suppose, General Grant, that the object of our

32 present meeting is fully understood. The terms I propose are those stated

33 . . . in my letter of yesterday.

Complete each statement below using the term "inside" or "outside."

1. Periods and commas are always placed _____ quotation marks.

2. An exclamation point or a question mark is placed _____ quotation marks when it punctuates the quotation or title.

3. An exclamation point or a question mark is placed _____ quotation marks when it punctuates the main sentence.

4. Semicolons and colons are always placed _____ quotation marks.

Parentheses, Ellipses, and Brackets

Ellipses are used to show the reader that some words are missing or to show a pause. Parentheses enclose explanatory or added material that interrupts the normal sentence structure. Brackets are used in quotations to clarify or show something added by someone other than the speaker. (See *Write Source,* pages 638, 642, and 644.)

> **Add** the correct punctuation to the sentences below.

1. "Because of the beautiful weather today, I know that many of you want me to keep my remarks brief I will." Cheers

2. Frank said the storm destroyed his house, wrecked his bike, crushed his watch But he was happy because no one was hurt.

3. The federal government banned the use of Freon although an excellent refrigerant because scientists showed this chemical was damaging the atmosphere's ozone layer.

4. Our school librarian said, "Gather everything books from the table."

5. The note was confusing. "Take three ears of corn and place an ear on each of the five *sic* tables in Room 225B."

6. Go to the building, collect five brushes, and bring them

7. The crater in Arizona one of the most incredible geologic events in the world was blasted into existence by a meteor.

8. Jimmy stunned everyone when he said, "The best way to defeat the pests black flies is cover yourself in bacon grease, so I did."

9. I quietly raised my camera slowly focused on the huge grizzly bear I waited I waited and got just the picture I wanted.

10. The coach called to his players, "You athletes the room was suddenly quiet are the finest sportsmen I have every known. Thank you!" applause

Pretest: Capitalization

Add the necessary capitalization to the following dialogue.

1   *O* ̷our history teacher, ms. radu, asked us if we could name the seven wonders

2   of the ancient world without looking in our book, *world history for everyone.*

3   just about everyone in world history 101 knew that the egyptian pyramids

4   at giza, egypt, had to be on the list. We had just read the chapter called

5   "egypt's mummies yield their secrets." dharma grant, the class brain, waved

6   her hand: "the hanging gardens of babylon are one of the ancient wonders," she

7   said. "they were built by king nebuchadnezzar II around 600 b.c.e. for his wife."

8   after thinking of only two answers, we were stumped; so ms. radu said

9   she'd give us a hint: "all of the wonders are found in the middle east, in

10   countries surrounding the mediterranean sea."

11   when she got no response, she asked, "don't any of you remember learning

12   greek and roman mythology in junior high? who was the father of the greek

13   gods? surely, someone knows that answer."

14   from the back of my brain, I dredged up a name that had lodged there

15   during my days at grover cleveland junior high school. "zeus!" I exclaimed. "he

16   was the king, or something."

17   "exactly," said Ms. radu. (she was trying to keep from smiling.) "The

18   statue of zeus, at olympia, greece, is the third ancient wonder." Then she told us

19   the other four places: a lighthouse at alexandria, egypt; a temple at ephesus,

20   turkey; a statue on the island of rhodes; and a mausoleum (that's a large tomb)

21   in turkey.

22 "why isn't the great wall of china on the list?" someone asked. "my father

23 said it's one of the only things on earth that you can see from outer space."

24 "great question," ms. radu replied. "how about someone from the smithville

25 science club answering that one."

26 "maybe they didn't know about it," briana jones said. "china is much

27 farther east than the middle east, and at&t wasn't around back then."

28 "brilliant," ms. radu said. "but now let's do a u-turn and think about today's

29 world. What are the most amazing structures in the modern world? And don't

30 give me any lame answers like the smithville baptist church or the

31 headquarters for the smithville democratic club."

32 we came up with the highest buildings in the world, the petronas towers in

33 kuala lumpur, malaysia, and famous places where people worship, such as st.

34 peter's basilica in rome.

35 other students said they thought that natural wonders were greater than

36 those made by human hands and named the himalayan mountains in tibet and

37 the grand canyon in the united states to make their point.

38 howard meyerhoff said that a simple a-frame home could be as beautiful as

39 some ancient temple or modern skyscraper, but that's the kind of weird answer

40 you can expect from howard—summer, winter, spring, or fall.

Capitalization 1

Proper names are always capitalized, as are the following:

> races (**Hispanic**), nationalities (**French**), languages (**Swahili**), and religions (**Hinduism**)

> organizations (**Lions Club**), associations (**World Soccer Federation**), and teams (**Milwaukee Mustangs**)

> titles (**Mrs.**) and acronyms (**NAACP**)

> letters used to indicate shape and form (**T-shirt**).

Turn to 648.1, 650.5, 650.6, or 652.2–652.4 in *Write Source* for more information and examples.

Place capital letters wherever they are needed.

1. $\overset{S}{\cancel{s}}$enator susan ricketts, my father's classmate and neighbor, was a republican first, but then made a u-turn and became a democrat.

2. At greenfield high school, she had the lead role in *my fair lady*.

3. she began her ascent as a star center fielder for the greenfield super slugs.

4. in college, she met a lot of future campaign volunteers through the young republicans, amnesty international, and the toastmasters club.

5. while still in college, she wrote two books: *how to speak knowledgeably about gravy* and *a college student's economic reform efforts*.

6. Her father encouraged her to study for her ph.d., which she did—specializing in international affairs.

7. She took the ricketts name when she married her husband.

8. when i see her, i teasingly call her "senator dr. mrs. ricketts."

9. she replies, "i have more titles than the greenfield public library."

10. she speaks spanish, french, and english and can make an audience laugh in all three languages.

Extend: Try writing a few sentences about what you plan to do in the next 5 to 10 years. Be serious or silly, but use many examples of proper capitalization.

Capitalization 2

The following words are capitalized:

> names for the Supreme Being (God, Allah, Jehovah); the names for holy books, such as the Bible, the Koran, and the Talmud

> days of the week, the months, holidays and holy days (Christmas, Hanukkah, Kwanza)

> trade names (Ford trucks)

> periods and events in history (the Renaissance, Battle of Normandy); political parties (Democratic Party, Libertarian Party)

Turn to 648.1 and 650.5 in *Write Source* to review capitalization rules.

Place capital letters wherever they are needed.

1. *T*
   the mesozoic period came after the permian era according to our science teacher, dr. samuelson.

2. it didn't matter what people were—democrat, republican, independent—everyone was shocked when president kennedy was assassinated.

3. grandma edith believes in god, grandma katherine believes in allah, and great-aunt tilly believes in buddha.

4. kelty's birthday is october 13, which sometimes falls on a friday.

5. i'm afraid joel will miss the republican reform party's rally on saturday since he'll be honoring rosh hashanah.

6. did any of the men who signed the declaration of independence suffer consequences?

7. my neighbor raquel zeneh ran for a seat in the house of representatives on the libertarian party platform.

8. The national aeronautics and space administration (nasa) maintains the dryden flight research center at edwards air force base in california.

Extend: For each capitalization error you made in this activity, write two sentences containing correct examples of that rule.

Capitalization 3

Turn to 648.1–652.5 in *Write Source*.

> **Place** capital letters wherever they are needed.

1. The ~~a~~*A*uburn university tigers play the university of washington huskies monday.

2. President reagan probably never considered joining the libertarian party.

3. I wonder if the magna carta was signed on a tuesday or a wednesday.

4. The new england patriots' home stadium is located in a suburb of boston.

5. Christians celebrate jesus christ's birth in december.

6. This year, the chinese new year will be celebrated in early february.

7. Sam will take uncle charlie to an african storytelling performance next sunday.

8. Joey says it's un-american to eat a hot dog without mustard.

9. The chief engineer does not know why the mars climate orbiter was lost.

10. It happened when they shot the satellite into orbit around mars.

11. How well can you see the milky way from alaska?

12. About 165,000 native hawaiians live in hawaii, the aloha state.

13. Turn north at first american bank.

14. Have you read the book *angela's ashes* by frank mcCourt?

15. Many egyptians are muslims; they practice the islamic religion.

16. My grandparents, who go to florida for the winter, are called "snowbirds" by the people who live in the south.

17. Professor girell, who lives next door, teaches religious subjects, and he has studied the bible, the koran, and the talmud.

18. His home is located on sugarloaf road, not park lane.

Extend: For each capitalization error you made in this activity, write two sentences containing correct examples of that rule.

Review: Capitalization

Correct the capitalization in the following student writing.

1   *W*
          when i was a little boy, bunde, minnesota, was the cultural center of my

2   life. bunde was a tiny village planted beside minnesota highway 7, about 100

3   miles straight west of minneapolis. in fact, the village wasn't even a village;

4   the place consisted of eight houses, egbert foken's farm, a church, the

5   parsonage, and bunde cemetery.

6   my great-aunt, minnie (*aunt minkya* we called her), lived in a bulky

7   two-story house at the west end of bunde. aunt minnie's apple orchard stood

8   between her house and the little square home where grandma ulferts lived with

9   uncle harry, her 35-year-old son. just north of my grandma lived mrs. gruising;

10   and north of her lived mrs. bode with her 40-year-old son, clarence.

11   before he died, clarence's father, dr. bode, had been the minister at the

12   bunde christian reformed church, which was built next to his home and was

13   well-known for its christmas service. just east of the church, the bodies of

14   about 200 norwegian and german settlers rested beside dr. bode under the tall

15   trees and thick sod in the church cemetery. south of the cemetery, mrs. alberts

16   lived behind a screen of long-haired willow trees and thick honeysuckle—all of

17   which hid her tiny chicken coop and the old, steep-roofed, pale green house that

18   looked like a cuckoo clock.

19   each day, in cars and trucks on minnesota highway 7, hundreds of

20   strangers shot through that little gathering of trees and buildings and

21   gravestones. i suspect that few of them realized that the blur they saw was

22   really the cultural oasis for our farm community.

Numbers 1

Depending on the situation, numbers are represented by words or numerals. Business, scientific, legal, and technical writings tend to use numerals. In other areas, numbers are often written out. Become familiar with the basic guidelines in *Write Source,* covering the most common ways to use numbers. Turn to 658.1–658.4 in *Write Source.*

Underline each misused number and write the correction above it.

1. Halley's comet is named after the English astronomer Edmund Halley, who

   observed it in <u>sixteen eighty-two.</u>
   1682

2. It takes Halley's comet about seventy-five years to complete its orbit and return

   to our skies.

3. For the last two thousand years, it has followed this schedule.

4. The most recent passing of Halley's comet took place February ninth,

   nineteen eighty-six.

5. The European Space Agency's *Giotto,* a satellite, once came within

   six hundred and five kilometers of the comet.

6. Halley's comet appears to rotate on its axis once every two point two days.

Use numbers to demonstrate each rule that is listed below.

1. You may use a combination of numerals and words for very large numbers.

   _____

2. Numbers being compared or contrasted should be kept in the same style.

   _____

3. If time is expressed in words, spell out the number.

   _____

Extend: Write sentences for the following: (1) Start a sentence with your age. (2) Include the date and year of your birth in another sentence. (3) In one more sentence, include the time you eat dinner and how much time you usually spend eating.

Numbers 2

Regardless of size, numbers are always spelled out at the beginning of a sentence and on the center line of a personal check. Numbers used in the same way should be treated the same way—all should be either written as words or written as numbers. (The three cats, two dogs, and fifty mice ate 20 cans of food. *Notice that* cans *represents a new category, so the numeral* 20 *is used.*) Turn to 658.1–658.4 in *Write Source.*

> **Underline** each misused number and write the correction above it.

1. The Colosseum in Rome is an immense superstructure that stands <u>forty-nine</u> *49*

   meters high and covers an area one hundred eighty-nine meters long and

   one hundred fifty-six meters wide.

2. Construction of the Colosseum began in sixty-nine C.E. and was completed in

   eighty C.E.

3. 76 of the Colosseum's 80 bays served as entryways.

4. The outer wall had 4 stories and could accommodate fifty thousand spectators.

5. The arena measured eighty-six meters by fifty-four meters.

> **Use** the following numbers in sentences that demonstrate the rule that is listed.

1. (2, 9) Numbers from one to nine are usually written as words.

   _____

2. (99) Use words to express numbers that begin a sentence.

   _____

3. (15) If numbers are used infrequently in a piece of writing, you may spell out
   those that can be written in one or two words.

   _____

Extend: Write sentences that correctly demonstrate the use of numbers for the three exceptions listed at 658.1 in *Write Source.*

Abbreviations

Abbreviations are used to shorten a word or phrase. Too many abbreviations (or abbreviations that are not clearly explained) can confuse a reader. Turn to pages 660–662 in *Write Source*.

Spell out the following abbreviations.

1. NE _northeast_

2. COD _____

3. dept. _____

4. CDT _____

5. qt _____

6. Ore. _____

7. etc. _____

8. ed. _____

9. MS _____

10. g _____

Abbreviate the following words and phrases.

1. Colorado _CO (or) Colo._

2. cup _____

3. incorporated _____

4. that is _____

5. Internal Revenue Service _____

6. please reply _____

7. kilogram _____

8. Illinois _____

9. population _____

10. percent _____

List three acronyms and three initialisms that you want to learn. Include the phrases they represent. Turn to page 662.

Acronyms	**Initialisms**
1. _____	1. _____
2. _____	2. _____
3. _____	3. _____

Extend: Look through one or two of your textbooks from another class, searching for abbreviations, acronyms, and initialisms. Write them down. Exchange lists with a classmate to see how many each of you can identify.

Review: Numbers & Abbreviations

> **Underline** any number or abbreviation used incorrectly and write the correction above. Finally, answer the questions.

1. The top secret Manhattan Project was begun <u>6/9/42</u>. *June 9, 1942*

2. Adolf Hitler and the Nazis were winning WW II. The U.S. and its allies needed a powerful weapon to stop them.

3. Albert Einstein and other scientists worked with the Corps of Engineering to help develop a nuclear bomb ASAP.

4. 3,000 people living in the Oak Ridge, TN, area were relocated to make way for 3 supersecret military factories.

5. Speed was necessary, so contractors had to build prefabricated homes for the workers, sometimes in less than an hr.

6. Anyone over the age of 12 did not enter or leave the city without her or his security badge and personal identification number (PIN).

7. Today, Oak Ridge manufacturers produce heat-resistant ceramics that protect space shuttles up to twenty-three thousand °F.

8. Some thirty-four thousand ceramic tiles are used as heat shields on the shuttle.

9. Superconductor ceramics are also helping to create "floating" trains that will travel two hundred to three hundred mph.

10. How do you present numbers that begin a sentence?

   _____

11. How do you express time with either A.M. or P.M.?

   _____

12. How do you express the numbers 10 and above?

   _____

Pretest: Plurals & Spelling

> **Write** the correct spelling above each underlined word that is misspelled. Write **C** above each underlined word that is spelled correctly.

1　Peanut butter and jelly *sandwiches* sandwichs are almost an American institution.

2　Maybe you're one of the unfortunates who steers away from peanut butter

3　because you think it's too fatening. Take note: Studys at Harvard University

4　show that peanut butter can be part of a sucesful weight-loss program because

5　peanut butter satisfies the appetite. It's the happyness factor. You eat less

6　because you feel full.

7　Who were the geniusses who "invented" PB&J sandwiches? We'll probably

8　never know, but if they could have patented their invention, they could be

9　enjoying lifes of luxury now.

10　There are approximatly 850 peanuts in every 18-ounce jar of peanut butter.

11　I'd say our family goes thru at least one jar a week, so in a year—let me see—

12　that would be 52 jarsful of peanut butter and 44,200 peanuts! Where do they

13　all come from?

14　Peanuts have a gloryous, multicultural past. They originated in the

15　Western Hemisphere, most likly in Brazil, and were domesticated in anceint

16　times by Native Americans in both North and South America. Of course, all

17　schoolchildrens learn about the contributions of George Washington Carver,

18　the African American sceintist who developed hundreds of uses for peanuts

19　and sweet potatos. But today, the two largest peanut-producing countrys in

20　the world are not even in the Western Hemisphere. China and India are the

21　front-runners in peanut production. (The United States, incidentaly, ranks

22　fifth.)

23   By high school graduation, the <u>avrage</u> American has eaten 1,500 peanut

24 butter sandwiches—many in their school <u>lunchs</u>. What are the <u>criteria</u> for a

25 great PB&J? If you limit yourself to peanut butter and grape jelly, you're being

26 too much of a <u>pureist</u>. Besides, what do you do when you discover that some

27 <u>realy</u> inconsiderate member of your family has used the last two <u>spoonsful</u> of

28 jelly in the jar and then set it back in the <u>refrigerator</u> without telling anyone?

29 <u>Necesity</u>, as they say, is the mother of invention. Honey or molasses will do

30 in a pinch, but the former is sticky and the <u>later</u> is runny. Applesauce, sliced

31 bananas, <u>pited</u> dates, chutney, and even dill pickles are favored by those with

32 <u>adventurous</u> (some would say <u>weird</u>) taste buds.

33   Restaurants that specialize in PB&J's are <u>croping</u> up across the country.

34 Most feature <u>loafs</u> of gourmet breads and peanut butter ground to your

35 <u>specifications</u>, like gourmet coffee. They should try adding <u>cinnamon</u> or raisins,

36 don't you think?

37   Let's face it—when you get down to everyday life, it's our <u>stomaches</u> that

38 do most of the talking. Right now, mine is reminding me of all those happy

39 <u>memorys</u> I have of eating <u>delishous</u> PB&J sandwiches. In my family, we

40 discovered what we <u>beleive</u> is an <u>improvment</u> on this great American staple.

41 Toast your PB&J as you would a <u>griled</u>-cheese sandwich. At our house, we

42 absolutely love them!

Plurals 1

The plurals of many nouns are formed by adding *s* to the singular, but there are some exceptions. *Remember:* A dictionary generally lists only irregular plural forms. If the plural form isn't listed, follow rules 654.1–656.4 in *Write Source.*

Write the plural of each word below. Consult a dictionary if necessary.

1. cupful *cupfuls* _____
2. disc _____
3. alley _____
4. buoy _____
5. radio _____
6. self _____
7. lunch _____
8. jeep _____
9. melody _____
10. soprano _____
11. leaf _____
12. reef _____
13. beach _____
14. typist _____
15. injury _____
16. potato _____
17. puff _____
18. wharf _____
19. child _____
20. gentleman _____

21. fistful _____
22. ox _____
23. tankful _____
24. louse [the insect] _____
25. grandchild _____
26. antenna _____
27. mouthful _____
28. fungus _____
29. phenomenon _____
30. brother-in-law _____
31. chief of protocol _____
32. agency _____
33. wolf _____
34. hairdo _____
35. trolley _____
36. tomato _____
37. maid of honor _____
38. editor in chief _____
39. mosquito _____
40. echo _____

Extend: Write five sentences using the plurals that give you the most difficulty.

Plurals 2

The plurals of many nouns are formed by adding *s* to the singular, but there are some exceptions. Turn to 654.1–656.4 in *Write Source*.

> **Write** the correct plural above each underlined noun.

1. Logging <u>camp</u> *camps* in northern Minnesota, Wisconsin, and Michigan contained colorful <u>person</u> who lived colorful <u>life</u>.

2. The camps were exciting <u>place</u> to live, but <u>job</u> were demanding, and <u>day</u> were long.

3. The <u>logger</u> often used <u>river</u> to transport the cut <u>log</u> from the <u>forest</u> to the <u>sawmill</u>.

4. Sometimes the limbless tree <u>trunk</u> would get jammed up in a river bend, resulting in <u>logjam</u> that explosives <u>expert</u> had to clear with dynamite.

5. It took many people to run a logging camp; for instance, <u>feeder</u> or barn <u>boss</u> would feed the <u>horse</u> and clean the <u>barn</u>.

6. <u>Blacksmith</u> made and fitted <u>horseshoe</u>; they also made or repaired iron <u>part</u> for <u>sleigh</u>, <u>wagon</u>, and other equipment.

7. Bull <u>cook</u> (also called barroom <u>man</u> or chore <u>boy</u>) filled the wood <u>box</u>, swept the <u>bunkhouse</u>, and fed the <u>pig</u>.

8. <u>Clerk</u> worked in the <u>store</u> or managed the <u>wanigan</u> (supply chests or storage <u>shack</u> on wheels).

9. They ordered <u>supply</u>; the <u>5</u>, <u>18</u>, or <u>28</u> in their <u>record</u> were often impossible to decipher.

10. "Cruiser" (also called <u>estimator</u>, <u>land looker</u>, or <u>valuer</u>) estimated the value of the standing timber.

Extend: Make a list of plural words that are correct examples of the one rule (654–656) that causes you the most difficulty.

Spelling 1: *i* before *e*

Write *i* before *e* except after *c,* or when sounded like *a* as in *neighbor* and *weigh*. Eight exceptions to this rule are included in the following sentence: Neither sheik dared leisurely seize either weird species of financiers. Additional exceptions are *their, height, counterfeit, heir,* and *foreign*. Turn to 664.1 in *Write Source.*

> **Fill** in the blanks below with the correct spelling of each word.

Write *i* before *e* . . .

1. f—ld *field* _____

3. br—f _____

2. rel—f _____

4. p—ce _____

except after *c,*

1. conc—ve _____

2. dec—ve _____

or when sounded like *a* as in *neighbor* and *weigh*.

1. fr—ght _____

3. w—ght _____

2. v—n _____

4. r—gn _____

> **Fill** in the blanks, writing the correct spelling of each word using *ie* or *ei.*

1. If you want to *(rec—ve)* _____ *receive* _____ a passing grade in English,

you must work hard on your spelling.

2. If you *(bel—ve)* _____ that good spelling is unnecessary these

days, you are only *(dec—ving)* _____ yourself.

3. You would probably also trust in the little red-suited elf who rides in a

(sl—gh) _____ pulled by *(—ght)* _____

tiny *(r—ndeer)* _____ .

4. Learning how to *(ach—ve)* _____ in spelling is not easy.

5. There are several important steps you must learn to follow if you are to become

a heavy*(w—ght)* _____ in the sport of spelling.

Writers INC 516.1

6. First of all, you must learn to be *(pat—nt)* _____ ; good

spelling takes time.

7. Second, you must check the correct pronunciation of each word you are

attempting to learn. A dictionary is the best *(fr—nd)* _____

to consult for word pronunciation.

8. As you are checking your dictionary, take a *(br—f)* _____

look at the meaning and history of each word. This information will help you

recall the spelling of the word because you can now *(perc—ve)* _____

where and how this word might be used.

9. Before you close the dictionary, look away from the page and try to *(v—w)*

_____ , or see, each word in your mind. Write the word on your

paper using only your mind's eye for *(conc—ving)* _____ the

proper spelling.

10. Learn some spelling rules. You should begin by *(s—zing)* _____

the opportunity to learn the four rules presented in *Write Source.*

11. Use memory techniques to *(retr—ve)* _____ the correct

spelling for words you use often.

12. Make a list of the words you misspell and *(rev—w)* _____

them as often as you can. Use the tips we just covered. Your spelling will begin

to *(y—ld)* _____ better grades and pride in yourself.

Extend: Memorize the sentence containing exceptions to the "*i* before *e*" rule. (Neither sheik dared leisurely seize either weird species of financiers.) Write it without looking at the original. Then check your spelling.

Spelling 2: Consonant Endings

If the last syllable of a word is accented when spoken aloud, the spelling rule for doubling consonants may apply. Study rule 664.2 in *Write Source,* but always check your dictionary for exceptions.

> **Write** an accent mark above the stressed syllable in each word below. If you are unsure, say the word aloud or check a dictionary.

1. omit´	**6.** refer	**11.** cover	**16.** gallop
2. linger	**7.** concur	**12.** commit	**17.** occur
3. differ	**8.** honor	**13.** control	**18.** murmur
4. forget	**9.** begin	**14.** equip	**19.** admit
5. regret	**10.** confer	**15.** prefer	**20.** humor

> **Add** the suffix *able, ing,* or *ed* to each word below. Use each suffix at least four times.

1. omit *omitted*	**8.** honor _____	**15.** prefer _____
2. linger _____	**9.** begin _____	**16.** gallop _____
3. differ _____	**10.** confer _____	**17.** occur _____
4. forget _____	**11.** cover _____	**18.** murmur _____
5. regret _____	**12.** commit _____	**19.** admit _____
6. refer _____	**13.** control _____	**20.** humor _____
7. concur _____	**14.** equip _____	**21.** color _____

> **Add** one of the following suffixes to each word below: *ence/ance, ent/ant,* or *er.*

1. concur *concurrent*	**5.** refer _____	**9.** color _____
2. wrap _____	**6.** bat _____	**10.** quit _____
3. occur _____	**7.** differ _____	**11.** stop _____
4. admit _____	**8.** flip _____	**12.** control _____

Writers INC 516.2

Spelling 3: Silent *e*

If a word ends with a silent *e*, drop the *e* before adding an ending that begins with a vowel. Do not drop the *e* when adding a suffix that begins with a consonant. Exceptions to the silent *e* rule occur when the final *e* is preceded by either *c* or *g*, and these exceptions are true only when adding *able* or *ous*. (*Truly, awful,* and *argument* are additional exceptions. Turn to 664.3 in *Write Source.*)

> state—stating—statement   > like—liking—likeness

> **Combine** the following words with the suffixes listed. Remember both the silent *e* rule and the exceptions.

1. nature + al _natural_

2. nine + ty _____

3. store + age _____

4. true + ly _____

5. guide + ance _____

6. peace + able _____

7. lone + ly _____

8. advise + able _____

9. sense + less _____

10. desire + able _____

11. state + ment _____

12. fame + ous _____

13. excite + ment _____

14. hope + less _____

15. lone + some _____

16. care + less _____

17. safe + ty _____

18. nerve + ous _____

19. live + able _____

20. arrive + al _____

> **Add** the suffix *ing* to each of the following words. Again, remember the rule.

1. come + ing _coming_

2. hope + ing _____

3. use + ing _____

4. argue + ing _____

5. ache + ing _____

6. believe + ing _____

7. love + ing _____

8. divide + ing _____

9. feature + ing _____

10. lose + ing _____

Spelling 4: Final *y*

When *y* is the last letter in a word and it is preceded by a consonant, change the *y* to *i* before adding a suffix (unless the suffix itself begins with an *i*). Turn to 654.3 and 664.4 in *Write Source*.

> **carry—carrier—carrying**

> **reply—replied—replying**

Combine the following words and suffixes. Remember: Do not change *y* to *i* if *y* is preceded by a vowel.

1. beauty + ful *beautiful*

2. easy + ly _____

3. marry + age _____

4. journey + s _____

5. chimney + s _____

6. monkey + ed _____

7. hungry + er _____

8. turkey + s _____

9. employ + er _____

10. hurry + ed _____

11. try + ing _____

12. lady + es _____

Combine the words and suffixes below.

1. busy + ly *busily*

2. destroy + ed _____

3. library + es _____

4. territory + al _____

5. ready + ness _____

6. diary + es _____

7. lovely + est _____

8. ninety + es _____

9. twenty + eth _____

10. attorney + s _____

11. bury + ed _____

12. safety + es _____

13. annoy + s _____

14. sully + es _____

15. necessary + ly _____

16. likely + hood _____

17. secretary + al _____

18. vary + able _____

19. defy + ance _____

20. scrappy + ness _____

Add the missing letter: either *y* or *i*.

1. hill_*i*_ness

2. var__ous

3. dela__ed

4. merc__ful

5. funn__est

6. bab__ish

7. fur__ous

8. bur__al

9. carr__ing

Combine each word below with the suffix listed beside it.

1. The dictionary defines a *contest* as "a struggle for superiority or victory." *Vary +*

   ous _____Various_____ words describe such struggles more precisely.

2. A boxing contest, for example, is called a *bout*. So is a struggle with an illness.

   Neither situation is very *enjoy + able* _____ , and *bout*

   convey + s _____ this better than the word *contest*.

3. When two political candidates "struggle for victory," the contest is called

   a *campaign*. Campaigns are also *employ + ed* _____ in

   warfare. Either way, the struggle is usually *fury + ous* _____

   and *weary + some* _____ .

4. Politicians combat their *adversary + es* _____ with words.

   When words fail, soldiers *battle* their *enemy + es* _____ with

   deadlier weapons. The political struggle is called a *debate;* the military struggle

   is called a *skirmish,* a *confrontation,* a *battle,* a *campaign,* or a *war*.

Extend: If a word has only one syllable, the final *y* is not changed when adding either *ly* or *ness*. Combine the words and suffixes below.

1. shy + ness _*shyness*_____

2. pretty + ly _____

3. sly + ly _____

4. dry + ness _____

Review: Plurals & Spelling

Complete each word below by adding either *ei* or *ie*.

1. w_*ei*_ght

2. ch____f

3. v___w

4. dec____ve

5. r____gn

6. n____ghbor

7. y____ld

8. fr____nd

9. for____gn

Place accent marks in the underlined word below. Then add the suffix listed.

1. prefer´ + ed *preferred* _____

2. omit + ed _____

3. admit + ance _____

4. forget + ful _____

5. equip + ed _____

6. control + ing _____

7. regret + able _____

8. counsel + ed _____

9. begin + ing _____

10. differ + ing _____

Combine the following words with the suffixes listed.

1. lone + ly *lonely* _____

2. desire + able _____

3. care + less _____

4. store + age _____

5. safe + ty _____

6. true + ly _____

7. fame + ous _____

8. guide + ance _____

9. argue + ing _____

10. lose + ing _____

11. lone + some _____

12. nine + ty _____

13. use + ing _____

14. live + able _____

15. state + ment _____

16. peace + able _____

Combine the words and suffixes below.

1. easy + ly _easily_____
2. journey + s _____
3. bury + ed _____
4. library + es _____

5. mercy + ful _____
6. lucky + ly _____
7. turkey + s _____
8. chimney + s _____

Make the following words plural. Some have irregular spellings.

1. wife _wives_____
2. belief _____
3. knife _____
4. roof _____
5. wolf _____
6. chief _____
7. cliff _____
8. child _____
9. ox _____
10. mouse _____
11. goose _____
12. tooth _____
13. woman _____
14. syllabus _____

15. thief _____
16. fife _____
17. life _____
18. loaf _____
19. strife _____
20. puff _____
21. elf _____
22. editor in chief _____
23. son-in-law _____
24. runner-up _____
25. drive-in _____
26. lean-to _____
27. two-year-old _____
28. vertebra _____

Pretest: Using the Right Word

> **Write** the correct word above each underlined word that is used incorrectly.

1   Accept for ringing my hands nervously, I stood stationery behind the heavy

2   velvet curtain. Each second past as slowly as an hour, but my heart beat faster

3   then a drumroll until I thought my vanes would pop. I came up with a plan to

4   run backstage, lay down, and send out anyone beside me to play my part.

5   Its almost like Ms. Keadon, the director, herd what I was thinking. She

6   wasn't about to let me alone. Before I got any further, she spun me around, and

7   firmly brought me back to my mark.

8   As a moral boost she whispered, "It's all right. You are going to be real

9   great. You can led this play. Now go out there and brake a leg!"

10   I knew she was inferring that she choose me to play the principle role in

11 the play because she believed in me. That was quite a complement, but how

12 could I do good if I couldn't remember the first line? Why did I want this part

13 so bad anyways? Was I under the allusion that acting was all about having fun

14 and waring beautiful costumes? Had I forgotten how shy I am?

15   I panicked. Then I thought of all the hours Ms. Keadon would learn me

16 and the other cast members our lines. I couldn't dessert them now. During

17 every rehearsal Ms. Keadon had treated us as professionals, and it was time I

18 started to act as one. It was my moment, and I was ready.

Using the Right Word 1

Words convey our thoughts to other people, so we need to be sure the right words are being used. Turn to pages 678–680 in *Write Source* for more information.

> **Underline** the correct word from the pair in parentheses in the following sentences.

1. Although many people *(accept, except)* the giant sequoia as the oldest tree in the world, most scientists agree that the bristlecone pine actually holds the record.

2. Most bristlecone pines live to be about 1,000 years old, but a *(amount, number)* of them are easily 3,000 years old or older.

3. *(Among, Between)* these older trees is Methuselah thought to be the oldest living thing on earth at 4,723 years.

4. Using a core sample taken of that tree, researchers can see the yearly growth and count the *(annual, biannual, biennial)* growth rings.

5. The *(base, bass)* or the trunk of the tree is secured to a mountainside by several strong roots.

6. As a result, very *(bad, badly)* weather rarely causes serious damage to the tree.

7. Weather does *(affect, effect)* the size and shape of these trees, however.

8. *(Beside, Besides)* being twisted and gnarled, bristlecone pines rarely reach 60 feet; most of them are much shorter than that.

9. *(Already, All ready)* at a young age these trees are forced by the power of the wind and the low moisture levels to grow slowly and close to the ground.

10. The *(bad, badly)* warped tree grows thick bark resistant to disease and puts out needles that last almost 40 years.

11. A bristlecone's appearance gives the *(allusion, illusion)* of dead driftwood.

12. A careful study of the bristlecone pine will show that it is *(alright, all right)*.

13. *(Anyway, Anyways)*, the bristlecone pine is a survival expert.

Extend: Write a sentence for each of the following words: *effect, except, badly,* and *besides.*

Using the Right Word 2

The following exercise uses some words that sound or look like other words and are often used incorrectly. Turn to pages 682–684 in *Write Source* for more information.

> **Check** each underlined word. If it is wrong, write the correct word above it.

1   The 10th-grade student <u>counsel</u> would like to announce this year's

2   Homecoming float contest. Last year, Kisha Morgan's winning float idea struck

3   a <u>cord</u> with the judges, who <u>choose</u> our float for the second-place spot. That was

4   a huge <u>complement</u>. This year, our talents will <u>bring</u> us even <u>farther</u>, so we <u>may</u>

5   <u>brake</u> the winning streak of the senior class.

6   <u>Chose</u> your best idea and <u>bring</u> it to the school office drop box by the end

7   of the day on October 9th. Student <u>counsel</u> will <u>chose</u> the top three float entries

8   based on the following: how well the idea <u>compliments</u> the Homecoming theme,

9   creativity, and if we <u>may</u> build it in one week. A class vote on October 10th will

10   decide the winner.

11   Even if you don't <u>chose</u> to enter the contest, we'll need your help building

12   the float. The parade judges have put the <u>brakes</u> on help from parents. We can

13   get our parent's <u>council</u> on how to use tools, but they <u>can</u> not help us build the

14   float. When we need a <u>brake</u>, they can go to the Icy Freeze and <u>take</u> us some

15   root beer floats for <u>desert</u>!

Extend: Write sentences using these words: *counsel, break,* and *complement*. Ask a classmate to check your sentences.

Using the Right Word 3

Many words look or sound alike but have different meanings. They are often misused in conversation and in writing. Other words are somewhat similar in meaning, but are often used incorrectly. Turn to pages 686–688 in *Write Source* for help.

> **Check** each underlined word. If it is wrong, write the correct word above it.

1   The Gold Rush of 1848 <u>lead</u> many pioneers west, but there was also an

2   important group of people <u>immigrating</u> from the East. The Chinese had also

3   <u>herd</u> about the discovery of gold in the United States. California's nickname

4   became "Gold Mountain," <u>inferring</u> that there was enough gold for everyone

5   to do <u>good</u>. Just <u>as</u> countless others seeking a golden fortune, many Chinese

6   immigrants had to <u>let</u> their dreams on that "mountain," but they didn't give up

7   on the chance for a new life.

8   These hardworking immigrants did not <u>imply</u> from their disappointment

9   that they should return to China. At the time, China was largely under

10 Britain's control, and as a result, <u>it's</u> economy was suffering. That provided

11 motivation just <u>like</u> gold did.

12   Chinese immigrants did not <u>lay idol</u>. They <u>learned</u> themselves how to make

13 a living as gardeners, farmers, and merchants. In 1865, many would help to <u>lie</u>

14 hundreds of miles of railroad track for the Transcontinental Railroad project.

15 This would temporarily <u>led</u> them even farther east, but most returned to

16 California when the project was completed in 1869.

17   <u>Its</u> impossible to know how many people <u>immigrated</u> from China in search

18 of gold. However, <u>its</u> clear that the United States has one of <u>its</u> most valued

19 treasures not in gold, but in the Chinese immigrants who brought their hard

20 work, determination, and unique culture.

Using the Right Word 4

Some words that sound or look alike are often used incorrectly. Turn to pages 690–692 in *Write Source*.

> **Write** the correct word above each underlined word that is used incorrectly.

1   Many climbers have attempted to reach the <u>peek</u> of Mount Everest in

2   the <u>passed</u>, but few have succeeded. With one <u>peak</u> at the dangers of Everest,

3   most people's climbing <u>moral</u> plummets. For others, the challenge <u>peaks</u> their

4   interest. One of the <u>principle</u> factors that makes climbing Everest so difficult is

5   its elevation.

6   The higher the elevation, the less oxygen there is in the air. A lack of

7   oxygen can cause everything from <u>wringing</u> in the ears to extreme confusion.

8   The way down may be in <u>plain</u> sight, but confusion and exhaustion can cause

9   a climber to <u>set</u> down and freeze to death. That is why climbers depend on a

10   <u>morale</u> code. Climbers don't abandon their partners. At <u>real</u> high altitudes,

11   climbers may follow that <u>principal</u>, but they may be too weak to help.

12   The lack of water in the air and the hard work of climbing practically

13   <u>ring</u> the water out of a climber's body. Climbers <u>sit</u> cups filled with snow on

14   tiny stoves, but at high elevations it takes a <u>real</u> long time for the snow to melt.

15   Dehydration can also cause weakness and hazy thinking.

16   Everest's high elevation also creates strong winds and unpredictable

17   weather. As a result, the <u>peek</u> is too high for <u>plains</u> or helicopters to rescue

18   climbers in trouble. Sherpas are native climbing guides who often wear <u>plane</u>

19   clothing compared to the high-tech outfits of other climbers, but <u>passed</u> a

20   certain altitude even their bodies cannot adapt to Everest's extremes.

Extend: Write sentences using these words: *really, peek, passed.* Exchange papers with a classmate and check each other's work.

Writers INC pp. 529–530

Using the Right Word 5

Turn to pages 694–696 in *Write Source*.

> **Write** the correct word above each underlined word that is used incorrectly.

1   People have been trying to predict the <u>whether</u> for thousands of years,

2   although early methods depended more on folklore <u>then</u> science. Some people

3   claimed they could feel the coming <u>whether</u> in their <u>vanes</u>. Others believed the

4   <u>whether</u> depended on the <u>soles</u> of gods <u>whom</u> punished people with <u>vial</u> storms.

5   Advances in technology have made <u>whether</u> forecasts much more accurate.

6   <u>Whether</u> <u>veins</u> and barometers were <u>vary</u> helpful for making predictions

7   <u>wear</u> they were used. <u>Whether</u> <u>veins</u> showed changes in wind direction.

8   Barometers, <u>that</u> looked like glass <u>viles</u>, measured pressure changes in the

9   atmosphere. Used together, it was possible to predict the <u>whether</u> up to a day in

10   advance.

11   The telegraph enabled people to share <u>whether</u> data instantly. Before that,

12   people wrote about the <u>whether</u> on <u>stationary</u>, and sent the data by locomotive

13   to <u>who</u> it concerned. When it was received, it was usually old news. Forecasters

14   used telegraphs to quickly gather more data and <u>than</u> make predictions.

15   Today, worldwide data is collected and fed into super computers <u>which</u>

16   calculate the possibilities. Now people turn to <u>whether</u> forecasts to decide

17   <u>weather</u> or not to <u>ware</u> a jacket or bring an umbrella. However, even now, the

18   weather can <u>very</u> from the forecast. <u>Which</u> is because even a <u>sole</u> change in

19   the atmosphere can mean big <u>whether</u> changes. For now, long-term <u>whether</u>

20   predictions are in <u>vain</u>. Beyond a week in advance, forecasts are based more on

21   seasonal averages <u>then</u> actual predictions. The one thing that forecasters can

22   depend on is that <u>whether</u> is not <u>stationery</u>; it is always changing.

Review: Using the Right Word

Circle the correct choice in each set of words in parentheses.

1. I wanted to *(accept, except)* the invitation to the party; everyone *(accept, except)* Jaron was going.

2. During their date, Lake's *(compliment, complement)* to Hannah was the perfect *(compliment, complement)* to the evening.

3. *(Who, Whom)* else knows the person to *(who, whom)* you were speaking?

4. When Michael looked at the fine oak board, it was *(plain, plane)* to see that the *(plain, plane)* had gouged the wood.

5. Back *(than, then)* there were more laborers *(than, then)* managers.

6. Kadeem made some *(allusion, illusion)* to the fact that everything we were about to see would be an *(allusion, illusion)*.

7. The *(amount, number)* of trash left behind at the campground is directly related to the *(amount, number)* of people who stayed there.

8. We had done such a *(good, well)* job that our supervisor told us that if we did the next job just as *(good, well)*, she'd give us a day off!

9. *(Its, It's)* not beyond repair; all *(its, it's)* pieces are right there.

10. Just as Sam decided to *(lay, lie)* on the couch for a nap, his younger sister decided to *(lay, lie)* her big stuffed animal there.

11. *(Set, Sit)* that heavy box down. Then *(set, sit)* here and catch your breath.

12. The weather *(affects, effects)* a person's mood; seeing the sun after a week of rain can have an exhilarating *(affect, effect)*.

13. Upon *(farther, further)* examination, it appears the rat went *(farther, further)* into the maze than we originally thought.

    Writers INC pp. 523–532

14. Practice ran late, so I called to let my mom know that I was *(alright, all right)*.

15. Great-grandma Maria *(emigrated, immigrated)* from Peru after high school. She has never regretted *(emigrating, immigrating)* to this country.

16. Right before the accident, she hit the *(brakes, breaks)* as hard as she could. Her arm was badly bruised, but it didn't *(brake, break)*.

17. When did he stop playing football, *(anyway, anyways)*?

18. Marissa was *(all ready, already)* at the door before Hailey was *(all ready, already)* to go.

19. *(Among, Between)* the two of us, we both managed to fit in with the group and feel like we were *(among, between)* friends.

20. The judge felt *(bad, badly)* for the gymnast who fell off the balance beam, but had to give her a *(bad, badly)* score anyway.

21. The principal gave *(counsel, council)* to the student *(counsel, council)* president about the school dance.

22. I *(heard, herd)* the zoo keeper say that the new elephant in the zoo was welcomed by the *(heard, herd)*.

23. The Olympics *(peaked, peeked, piqued)* his interest at a very young age. He grinned as he *(peaked, peeked, piqued)* out from his red, white, and blue hooded jacket. The athlete knew that he was in *(peak, peek, pique)* condition for the race.

24. *(Base, Bass)* singers provide the *(base, bass)* for the chorus to build on.

25. Two people sat *(beside, besides)* me, but I felt like there wasn't anyone else in the room *(beside, besides)* Ben.

26. The stone *(idle, idol)* sat *(idle, idol)* among the other artifacts in the ancient ruins.

Review: Proofreading Activities

Write out the full word or phrase for these common abbreviations.

1. a.m. *before noon (ante meridiem)*   **6.** misc. _____

2. vs. _____   **7.** tbsp _____

3. oz. _____   **8.** r.s.v.p. _____

4. ex. _____   **9.** etc. _____

5. mdse. _____   **10.** pg. _____

Correct errors in punctuation, capitalization, spelling, plurals, numbers, and abbreviations in the sentences below. Write the corrections, when necessary, above the errors.

1. The Mount ~~r~~ushmore nat. mem. is located on Hwy. 16, 25 mi. s.w. of Rapid City, SD.

2. The heads of 4 U.S. Pres. are carved into the side of the mountain George Washington Thomas Jefferson Abraham Lincoln and Theodore Roosevelt.

3. These carveings are protected by the Nat. park Service and the Dept. of the interior.

4. The memorial can be veiwed 24 hrs. a day, 365 days a yr.

5. located in the black hills this mountain was chosen for its finely textured granite and the lack of viens showing thrughout the stone.

6. It also had the unusual feature of a smooth, three-hundred-foot perpendiculer face of granite on the e. side, perfect for carving.

7. On Aug. 10 1927 thousands watched as the artist and sculptor, Gutzon Borglum, made his decleration to begin construction.

8. a blacksmith shop, tool buildings, and artist studioes were built first.

9. Elaberate winches devices used for hauling or pulling were also constructed.

10. These held the workers in midair as they chiseled the enormus faces.

11. The lenth of Washington's nose is 20 ft; His head is the hieght of a 6-story building.

12. If he were carved from head to toe, he would be 140 m tall.

13. In order to get acurate mesurements, Borglum 1st carved a model.

14. A medal shaft was placed on the upper center of the models head.

15. A protractor was atached to the base of the shaft.

16. The angels were kept equal on both the model and the mountain, while the lenths were measurred in a ratio of 1 to twelve inches.

17. There were injurys during the hazzardous construction, but no deaths.

18. The most significant "injury" on the project was sufferred by Thomas Jefferson when an assistent used too much dynamite to create his outline.

19. As with a haircut, the artist can chisel granite here and there to "fix" the sculpture but unlike a haircut, granite does not grow back.

20. Jeffersons head was moved from Washington's right to his left. The last two presidents were compleeted w/o incedent.

21. Carving stoped in Oct. 1941, the eve of America's involvement in WW II.

22. The final dedication of the monnument occured 50 yrs. later, even though it was never completly finished.

23. The total construction cost was nearly $1000000, considerably more than Congress wanted to spend during the great depression.

24. Now, however, it is considerred a small price to pay for a unque memorial to those who shaped our histery.

Parts of Speech Activities

The activities in this section provide a review of the different parts of speech. Most of the activities also include helpful textbook references. In addition, the **Extend** activities encourage follow-up practice of certain skills.

Nouns   **73**

Pronouns   **80**

Verbs   **89**

Adjectives & Adverbs   **105**

Prepositions, Conjunctions, & Interjections   **113**

Parts of Speech Review   **119**

Pretest: Nouns

> **Underline** the words used as nouns in the following sentences.

1. Two <u>students</u>, Shannel Lumpkin and Monique Anderson, got a firsthand chance to learn about another culture.

2. Recently, they won all-expenses-paid trips to East Africa.

3. On their three-week journey, the two students from De LaSalle Education Center and their principal, Gayle Lee, visited the Masai Tribe and saw a snake farm.

4. They also spent time as guests of a family in Arusha.

> **Indicate** the function of each of the underlined nouns in the following sentences. Use **S** for subject, **PN** for predicate noun, **IO** for indirect object, **DO** for direct object, and **OP** for object of the preposition. Use **POS** for nouns showing ownership.

1. Both <u>students</u> are thankful for their <u>journey</u>.
(S) *(OP)*

2. They both felt that many things in <u>East Africa</u> were impressive.

3. For example, <u>East Africa's</u> young people show <u>elders</u> great <u>respect</u>.

4. Lumpkin and Anderson also noticed the <u>lack</u> of <u>materialism</u> and the safe <u>streets</u>.

5. The <u>experience</u> changed both <u>Lumpkin's</u> and <u>Anderson's</u> lives.

6. They say they gained <u>appreciation</u> for both <u>cultures</u>.

7. As this and other exchanges take place between <u>communities</u>, the <u>world</u> becomes a little smaller.

8. Such programs help people become a little more appreciative of their <u>differences</u> and <u>similarities</u>; the <u>world</u> becomes a <u>community</u>.

Types of Nouns

A common noun names a person, a place, a thing, or an idea. A proper noun names a *particular* person, place, thing, or idea. Proper nouns are capitalized. A collective noun refers to a group or a unit. For more information, turn to page 701 in *Write Source*.

> **Underline** the common nouns, capitalize the proper nouns, and write *COL* above the collective nouns in the following narrative.

1   For some reason, maps and I don't get along. Even folding the foolish

2   things correctly is an exercise in futility.

3   When it comes to directions, my family thinks I'm somewhere south of

4   uselessville as a navigator. My father says I cannot find my way out of a paper

5   bag, and sometimes I'm inclined to agree. My mother says, "Be kind. At least

6   he doesn't get lost in the neighborhood." I have a pair of brothers who are less

7   kind.

8   I think it's safe to say that I am not a descendant of magellan. Whether

9   I'm looking for a small shop or the main street cinema, you can be sure I will

10   find the most "scenic" route possible. Once while driving my friends to a movie,

11   I made a wrong turn. It took me an hour to find the right street again. What

12   an embarrassment!

13   To improve my cloudy sense of direction, I once enrolled in an orienteering

14   class in northwest montana. It didn't help. Luckily, I have no problem asking

15   people for directions. And upon my arrival—anywhere—I can always begin with

16   "A funny thing happened on my way. . . "

Extend: Think of a place you once visited. Describe that place to a friend in the form of a postcard. Exchange postcards with a classmate and underline all the nouns in each other's message.

Singular & Plural Nouns

Number indicates whether a noun is singular or plural. (You need to know the number of the noun you use as a subject, because the verb you choose must agree with that noun.) Turn to 702.1 in *Write Source*.

> **Write** an **S** above the underlined nouns that are singular and a **P** above the underlined nouns that are plural in the following sentences.

1. *P* <u>People</u> who live in an American <u>city</u> may live side by side with many <u>animals</u>.

2. <u>Birds</u> and <u>squirrels</u> are common, and you might even be able to find <u>deer</u> or coyotes.

3. But in other <u>parts</u> of the <u>world</u>, different animals are found on city <u>streets</u>.

4. In <u>Thailand</u>, thousands of wild monkeys live in <u>parks</u> and on rooftops.

5. Monkeys are sacred in the Buddhist <u>religion</u>, and for <u>hundreds</u> of years <u>monkeys</u> have been welcome in Thailand's Buddhist <u>temples</u>.

6. Once <u>cities</u> grew up around the <u>temples</u>, monkeys could no longer retreat to the <u>forest</u> and began to live alongside the city <u>dwellers</u>.

7. Most of the <u>monkeys</u> live quiet, peaceful <u>lives</u>, and some are even adopted as <u>pets</u>.

8. But some are very aggressive and will steal <u>ice cones</u> right out of people's <u>hands</u> as they exit convenience <u>stores</u>.

9. Luckily, only a few <u>people</u> are injured by monkeys each year—the monkeys are more <u>rascals</u> than <u>bullies</u>.

10. Each year, a <u>hotel</u> in one Thai city sets out a <u>feast</u> of fruit, rice, nuts, and candy for its primate <u>friends</u>.

11. For more information, see the January 1999 <u>issue</u> of *Smithsonian Magazine*.

Extend: For more practice distinguishing the number of a noun, turn to page 66 in the handbook. Ask a classmate to read the revised paragraph at the bottom of the page and pause after each noun, at which time you identify its number as singular or plural.

Functions of Nouns

Nouns can be used six different ways. Study the chart below and turn to *Write Source* for more information.

Writers INC	*Write Source*	Function	Symbol	Example
550.1	738.1	*subject*	**S**	*Burglars* steal.
534.3	702.3	*predicate noun*	**PN**	Burglars are *thieves*.
540.1	716.2	*direct object*	**DO**	Burglars steal your *possessions*.
540.1	716.2	*indirect object*	**IO**	Burglars gave *Grandpa* a scare.
547	732	*object of preposition*	**OP**	Burglars pried the jewels out of his *hands*.
534.3	702.3	*possessive noun*	**POS**	Burglars stole *Grandma's* jewelry.

> **Label** the function of each underlined noun in the following statements, using the symbols from the chart above.

                S   PN

1. Jade Snow Wong is a potter.

2. A potter is someone who shapes pottery by hand on a potter's wheel.

3. She was born in 1922 and grew up in Chinatown in San Francisco.

4. Jade Snow Wong's ability to make pottery made her father happy and her mother sad.

5. Jade has said, "Creativity is 90 percent hard work and 10 percent inspiration."

6. Wong gave her ordinary bowls beautiful glazes.

7. She wanted the dishes to be used every day.

8. When Jade Snow Wong and her glazed pots became famous, people's attitudes toward her changed.

9. In 1989, Jade Snow Wong wrote *Fifth Chinese Daughter,* her popular autobiography.

10. Later she became a highly regarded writer and an outstanding educator.

Extend: Write about a skill or talent you have. Use nouns and pronouns in all of the six ways. Ask a classmate to identify each of the nouns and pronouns you use.

Nominative, Possessive, & Objective Cases of Nouns

In the *nominative case,* a noun is used as the subject or the predicate nominative. In the *possessive case,* the noun shows ownership or possession. In the *objective case,* the noun is used as the direct object, the indirect object, or the object of a preposition. Turn to 702.3 in *Write Source.*

Writers INC	Write Source	Case	Function	Symbol	Example
550.1	738.1	Nominative	*subject*	**S**	The *car* wouldn't start.
534.3	702.3		*predicate noun*	**PN**	The car is a *lemon.*
540.1	716.2	Objective	*direct object*	**DO**	Jake gives me a *ride.*
540.1	716.2		*indirect object*	**IO**	Jake gives *me* a ride.
547	732		*object of preposition*	**OP**	He drives with *care.*
534.3	702.3	Possessive	*possessive noun*	**POS**	I appreciate *Jake's* driving.

Label the function of the underlined nouns in the following statements using the symbols from the chart above. Indicate the case of each underlined noun (**N** for nominative, **O** for objective, and **POS** for possessive) on the blanks.

___N___ **1.** Every year, wild and domestic animals _(S)_ kill about 200 Americans.

_____ **2.** Most people fear bears a great deal more than they fear deer.

_____ **3.** However, the bear's reputation as a killer is greatly exaggerated.

_____ **4.** Bears in America kill an average of one person a year.

_____ **5.** Even goats cause more deaths than that.

_____ **6.** Poisonous snakes and vicious dogs are certainly potential menaces.

_____ **7.** Sighting a shark gives most swimmers a fright.

_____ **8.** Stepping on a jellyfish's stinging tentacles is not a good idea.

_____ **9.** Desert hikers, especially, should know that a scorpion's sting can be fatal.

_____ **10.** Rattlesnakes also have a nasty reputation.

_____ **11.** Mosquitoes can be a nuisance, and occasionally do cause fatal diseases.

_____ **12.** But it's the mild-mannered deer that causes more than 130 deaths per year on the highways and back roads of America.

Extend: Write a short paragraph describing an unusual animal. Exchange papers with a classmate and identify the case of each noun. Discuss your answers and check your textbook to determine if your answers are correct.

Gender of Nouns

> **Underline** the nouns in the following sentences and put an *M, F, N,* or *I* above the nouns to indicate masculine, feminine, neuter, or indefinite. (See *Write Source*, page 702.)

1. *I*
   The best soccer <u>players</u> build up their stamina by running long distances.

2. Astronauts are willing to endure extremely uncomfortable and dangerous physical forces for the privilege of traveling into space.

3. Firemen represent one part of the group known as firefighters.

4. Flight attendants, once called stewardesses, help passengers have smooth, safe flights.

5. Actors and actresses must memorize not only lines but also actions.

6. Their father, who has years of experience, uses a band saw to build cabinets, tables, and dressers.

7. The mayor's niece visited five foreign countries this year.

8. Metal workers can hammer an ounce of gold into a 100-square-foot sheet or draw that same amount of gold into a wire 50 feet long.

9. Using binoculars, my uncle began to count the deer: three does, one buck, and four fawns.

10. When the senator stood up to speak, everyone groaned because they knew this would be a filibuster lasting at least a week.

11. The whale seemed to fly out of the water and, then it fell back with a gigantic splash thrilling the excited students and their teacher.

Review: Nouns

Function				Case		Number
subject	**S**	direct object	**DO**	nominative	**N**	singular
predicate noun	**PN**	indirect object	**IO**	objective	**O**	plural
object of preposition	**OP**	possessive	**POS**	possessive	**POS**	

Underline the nouns in the sentences below. Next, list them on the numbered lines in the same order that they appear in the sentences. Fill in the information required for each noun, using the symbols from the chart and words for *singular* and *plural.*

- Jack went to the concert with Maria's brothers.
- Our teachers gave my class many lectures about tardiness.
- Rosa is a renowned photographer.
- My cats' names are Hank and Maddie.

	NOUN	GENDER	FUNCTION	CASE	NUMBER
1.	Jack	M	S	N	singular
2.					
3.					
4.					
5.					
6.					
7.					
8.					
9.					
10.					
11.					
12.					
13.					
14.					

Pretest: Pronouns

> **Circle** the correct pronoun from the set in parentheses.

1. No astronauts have ever received more publicity than Neil Armstrong and Edwin "Buzz" Aldrin, for it was *(they,* *them)* who first walked on the surface of the moon.

2. Most of America watched *(they, them)* take the first moon walk on July 20, 1969.

3. How long will it be before some enterprising entrepreneur offers trips to the moon for people like you and *(I, me)*?

4. It was *(I, me)* who gave my brother, Aaron, a copy of Frommer's *The Moon: A Guide for First-Time Visitors.*

5. Now *(he, him)* and his friend Ahmed are planning their trip to the moon in their spare time.

6. I accidentally learned about their plans when I overheard *(he, him)* and Ahmed talking about it.

7. I believe my brother's personal conversation should be between *(he, him)* and his friend, but when it involves a trip to the moon, *(who, whom)* can resist listening?

8. Even though Aaron realized that the Frommer book is not completely serious, it obviously gave Ahmed and *(he, him)* their impossible idea.

9. I think Aaron *(himself, hisself)* would go tomorrow except for one thing: there are no flights available to civilians.

10. Between you and *(me, I)*, I think one of the big attractions of going to the moon for *(them, they)* is the possibility of doing spectacular flips and effortless slam dunks in low gravity.

Number & Person of Personal Pronouns

The *number* of a pronoun can be either singular or plural. The *person* of a pronoun indicates whether that pronoun is speaking *(I, we)*, is spoken to *(you)*, or is spoken about *(he, she, it)*. Turn to 708.1–708.2 in *Write Source* for more information and examples.

> **Write** sentences using personal pronouns as subjects. Use the number and person listed in the parentheses.

1. (first person, singular)

   I love to read books aloud to small children.

2. (third person, plural)

3. (second person, singular)

4. (first person, plural)

5. (third person, singular)

6. (second person, plural)

7. (first person, singular)

8. (third person, plural)

Extend: Without looking at your text, write out your own explanation of *number* and *person* of a pronoun. Use these words in your explanation: *singular, plural, first person, second person,* and *third person.*

Functions of Pronouns

Pronouns function the same way that nouns do. Study the chart below and turn to 710.1 in *Write Source*.

Writers INC	Write Source	Function	Symbol	Example
550.1	738.1	*subject*	**S**	*You* need to change your clothes.
538.1	710.1	*predicate noun*	**PN**	"That is *you*," she remarked about my shirt.
538.1	710.1	*direct object*	**DO**	The river's current pulled *him* under.
538.1	710.1	*indirect object*	**IO**	Frank gave *me* some paperback books.
547	732	*object of preposition*	**OP**	This isn't about *me*.
538.1	710.1	*possessive noun*	**POS**	*His* shoes were ruined by the rain.

> **Label** how the underlined pronouns function in the following statements, using the symbols from the chart above.

                     POS

1. Deciduous trees lose <u>their</u> leaves every autumn.

2. <u>They</u> are unlike coniferous trees in that respect.

3. <u>He</u> said the boy wouldn't go without <u>him</u>.

4. "I know <u>my</u> own weaknesses, and pizza is <u>one</u>," explained the man.

5. Maggie will drive <u>us</u> to the swim meet.

6. "<u>You</u> have to use <u>your</u> fingertips, not <u>your</u> palms," the volleyball coach advised.

7. Corinne did <u>me</u> a favor by making breakfast today.

8. The dog jumped on <u>her</u>, wagging <u>its</u> tail.

9. <u>My</u> lunch was missing, and <u>I</u> was mad.

10. Did <u>you</u> see <u>them</u> give the flowers to <u>her</u>?

11. <u>They</u> like to serve hominy to <u>their</u> guests.

12. <u>Your</u> mother gave <u>me</u> a sandwich.

13. "Did <u>they</u> find <u>it</u>?" asked Inez.

14. <u>Our</u> families take <u>their</u> vacations together.

Extend: Write your own sentences using pronouns in each of the six ways shown above.

Nominative, Possessive, & Objective Cases of Pronouns

The *case* of a personal pronoun is determined by how that pronoun is used in a sentence—as a subject, an object, or a possessive. Turn to 710.1 in *Write Source* for more information and examples.

> **Underline** the personal pronouns in the sentences below. Label the case of each pronoun. Use **N** for nominative case, **POS** for possessive case, or **O** for objective case.

      N   POS   O

1. He sold his bike to me last week.

2. You should play in our chess tournament because you're such a good competitor.

3. They need to give her a ride to her workplace.

4. Kendra and Leona came to our store so they could buy pet food.

5. The teacher expects a lot of you, Lisa.

6. When do you think Sara and Duncan will arrive at your home?

7. She will help you with your job search.

8. How did they find a song we both liked?

9. Maria, please let us know your arrival time.

10. Why did Jerry take his soccer ball home?

11. Jennifer gave me a copy of the CD.

12. Yang went out to move his car, but it was gone.

13. Is it time for us to eat dinner?

14. Have you ever heard him sing?

15. I saw the cat and brought it home.

16. Make her sandwich first.

17. They thanked me for my help.

18. Its climate was too damp for my health.

19. He and she will plan the schedule for us.

Extend: Choose six pronouns from the chart on page 710 in *Write Source*. Correctly use each one in a sentence.

Review: Pronouns 1

Underline the personal pronoun in each sentence below. In the first blank, indicate the number of the pronoun with **S** for singular or **P** for plural. In the second blank, identify the person with a **1, 2,** or **3** for first, second, or third person.

_P_ _1_ **1.** Last night <u>our</u> cat caught a mole in the backyard.

___ ___ **2.** Grandpa is taking us to see a movie at the new cinema.

___ ___ **3.** Justin, ask Grandpa if you can go along.

___ ___ **4.** They decided to buy a new car, after all.

___ ___ **5.** Did Dan invite all of you to join the office softball team?

___ ___ **6.** He plans to get shirts with the company logo.

Label the function of each underlined pronoun by writing the appropriate symbol above it. Use **S** for subject, **PN** for predicate nominative, **DO** for direct object, **IO** for indirect object, **OP** for object of a preposition, and **POS** for possessive. In the blanks below, indicate the case for each underlined pronoun by writing **N** for nominative, **O** for objective, and **P** for possessive.

_N_ ___ **1.** <u>It</u> is going to be a long day. *(S)*

___ ___ **2.** This magazine belongs to <u>me</u>.

___ ___ **3.** Would <u>you</u> like to borrow <u>it</u>?

___ ___ **4.** Sheila brought <u>them</u> bread that <u>she</u> had baked.

___ ___ **5.** <u>She</u> wants to use <u>my</u> colored pencils.

___ ___ **6.** <u>He</u> forgot <u>them</u>.

___ ___ **7.** When <u>you</u> finish cleaning the bathroom, help <u>me</u> vacuum.

___ ___ **8.** <u>My</u> mother planted 15 oak trees, but 6 of <u>them</u> died.

___ ___ **9.** <u>Our</u> teacher is <u>your</u> Grandma!

___ ___ **10.** <u>I</u> didn't know <u>their</u> house was robbed.

Relative Pronouns

A relative pronoun (*that, which, whose, who, whom*) relates an adjective clause to the noun or pronoun it modifies (as in "the team *who wins* . . . "). Turn to 706.2 and the chart on page 704 in *Write Source* for more information.

> **Underline** the relative pronouns in the sentences below. Circle the noun or pronoun that each relative pronoun modifies.

1. (Snakes,) <u>which</u> are limbless reptiles, have been feared by humans for centuries.

2. Those who do not take precautions around certain snakes could find themselves in real danger.

3. Snakes, which include about 2,400 different species, live almost everywhere on the planet.

4. The world's longest recorded snake was an Asiatic reticulated python that was more than 49 feet long.

5. Some snakes kill their prey by constriction, which does not crush the animal but suffocates it.

6. People who study snakes are called herpetologists.

7. Snakes whose venom is fatal to humans number fewer than 300 species.

8. The venom that snakes carry either destroys nerve cells or attacks blood tissue.

9. Most cobras, which live mainly in India, have poison that attacks the nervous system.

10. Humans, whom snakes avoid whenever possible, are among the most dangerous predators of snakes.

Extend: Write five sentences about reptiles. Use each of the five relative pronouns (listed at the top of this page) in adjective clauses. Turn to 612.2 in *Write Source* for helpful information about punctuating your clauses.

Writers INC 536.2, 535, and 491.2

Indefinite, Interrogative, & Demonstrative Pronouns

Indefinite pronouns represent someone (or something) not specifically named or known (*everybody, anyone, each*). Interrogative pronouns ask questions (*who? which? what?*). Demonstrative pronouns point out people or things without naming them (*this can't be, these are fine*). Turn to 706.3–706.5 in *Write Source* for more information.

> **Label** the underlined pronouns below. Use *I* for an indefinite pronoun, *D* for a demonstrative pronoun, and *IT* for an interrogative pronoun.

I

1   Almost <u>everyone</u> knows Ben Franklin was an inventor, a printer, a public

2   servant, and a writer. <u>Many</u> know that he proved lightning was caused by

3   electricity. <u>Some</u> know that he said, "Little strokes fell great oaks." But <u>who</u>

4   knows that he loved to read—especially books by John Bunyan, Plutarch,

5   Daniel Defoe, and Cotton Mather? <u>Those</u> were Franklin's favorites because he

6   said he learned so much from them.

7   <u>What</u> caused Franklin's formal schooling to end when he was 10 years old?

8   <u>That</u> happened largely because he was the 15th child in a family of 17, and his

9   father needed his help. <u>This</u> would seem to be a tragedy, and for <u>many</u> of us

10   it would be. But not for Franklin. <u>Nothing</u> would stop his education. He said,

11   "The doors of wisdom are never shut." Because of his positive attitude, Franklin

12   became <u>one</u> of the best-educated and most successful people of his time. <u>Which</u>

13   of his many successes was Franklin's greatest? <u>That</u> is hard to say.

14   <u>No one</u> would leave Franklin's name off a list of most famous Americans.

15   <u>Few</u> would leave his name off a list of the 10 most famous Americans. <u>Most</u> of

16   us recognize Franklin's face on coins, paper money, and postage stamps. <u>These</u>

17   are only a few ways that our country still honors this great man.

Extend: Write five sentences about some of Franklin's other accomplishments (developed a volunteer fire department, invented the Franklin stove and bifocals, and discovered that poorly ventilated rooms promote disease). Use an indefinite pronoun, an interrogative pronoun, and a demonstrative pronoun at least once.

Reflexive & Intensive Pronouns

Reflexive and intensive pronouns are formed by adding *-self* or *-selves* to personal pronouns (*myself, yourselves*). Turn to 706.1 in *Write Source* for definitions and examples.

> **Write** a sentence, changing the pronoun in parentheses to either a reflexive or an intensive pronoun.

1. (them) reflexive

   The paratroops called themselves Charlie Brown's Army.

2. (our) reflexive

_____

_____

3. (him) intensive

_____

_____

4. (it) intensive

_____

_____

5. (her) intensive

_____

_____

6. (your) reflexive

_____

_____

7. (my) reflexive

_____

_____

Extend: Choose two reflexive and two intensive pronouns. Use each in a sentence.

Review: Pronouns 2

> **Underline** the pronouns in the sentences below. On the lines write *relative, indefinite, interrogative, demonstrative, reflexive,* or *intensive* to identify each pronoun.)

intensive **1.** Joey can lift the boxes <u>himself</u>.

_____ **2.** This is not the meal that we ordered.

_____

_____ **3.** Who left a skateboard on the stairs?

_____ **4.** Mr. White said, "Give yourself a pat on the back."

_____ **5.** Jim's dog, Daisy, which saved our neighbor's cat, has been given an award.

_____ **6.** Jerry dragged himself to Grandma's house to mow the lawn.

_____ **7.** Everything is out of place in Leon's room.

_____ **8.** Lori visited the capitol, which has a bronze dome.

_____ **9.** What is Keiko doing with a 10-pound bag of potatoes?

_____ **10.** Is that the correct way to hold a hammer?

_____ **11.** Few understand the feeling of seasickness.

_____ **12.** Elena thinks the watch that was found crushed in the parking lot is Dan's.

_____ **13.** Which one do you want?

_____ **14.** Nobody in class could name every U.S. president.

_____ **15.** Derrick and Ron themselves cleaned the apartment before moving in.

Pretest: Verbs

Do the following three things for each sentence below: (1) underline all the main verbs once, (2) underline all the auxiliary (or helping) verbs twice, and (3) write the tense of each verb on the blank (*present, past, future, present perfect, past perfect,* or *future perfect*). Finally label each underlined verb as **A** for action, **L** for linking, or **H** for helping.

_____*past*_____ **1.** On August 17, 1999, a powerful earthquake _hit_ western Turkey.

_____ **2.** Before the sun came up that day, tens of thousands of

_____ sleeping people had been killed by the giant quake—a 7.4 on the Richter scale.

_____ **3.** Is the North Anatolian Fault in Turkey similar to the San Andreas Fault in California?

_____ **4.** Scientists have found them to be similar in size and have

_____ found movements in the tectonic plates to be similar.

_____ **5.** So-called "tectonic earthquakes" occur when the major and

_____ minor plates in the earth's crust move.

_____ **6.** Will scientists and engineers predict future earthquakes

_____ and prevent loss of life and property?

_____ **7.** In 1975, the Chinese accurately predicted a major

_____ earthquake at Haicheng and gave the city's residents

evacuation orders.

_____ **8.** The warning saved thousands of lives.

_____ **9.** Scientists now investigate bulges in land surfaces, changes

in the magnetic field, and even the behavior of animals.

_____ **10.** Is it possible that in the next 15 years earthquake

_____ prediction will have become more precise and reliable?

Types of Main Verbs

Verbs express action (*waved, wink, says*) or state of being (*is, are, be*) and serve as predicates in sentences. Both action verbs and linking verbs can serve as the main verb (without helping verbs) in a sentence. Turn to page 714.1 and 716.1 in *Write Source* for more information.

> **Underline** the main verbs in the following paragraphs.

1   Most Egyptians <u>live</u> near the Nile River or the Suez Canal, the country's

2   two major waterways. On the east bank of the Nile lies Cairo, Egypt's capital

3   and largest city. It overflows with people. About 7 million people reside in the

4   city of Cairo, but almost 13 million people live in the Cairo metropolitan area.

5   The people of Cairo cope with typical urban problems. Housing shortages

6   cause hardships. Many people crowd into small apartments or build makeshift

7   huts on roofs of apartment buildings or on land belonging to someone else.

8   Many live in poverty. Others enjoy modern conveniences and government

9   services. Extremes of wealth and poverty can be seen in Cairo and other

10 Egyptian cities. Attractive residential areas exist beside vast slums. Some of

11 the poorest people in Cairo take refuge in historic tombs on the city's outskirts

12 in an area known as the City of the Dead.

13   Cairo's Al-Azhar University was founded in 970 C.E. and is one of the

14 world's oldest universities. It serves as the world's leading center of Islamic

15 teaching. About 90 percent of the Egyptians practice Islam, the Muslim religion.

16 Islam influences family life, social relationships, business activities, and

17 government affairs. Muslims pray five times daily, give money or products to

18 the poor, fast, and, if possible, make a pilgrimage to Mecca, Saudi Arabia, the

19 sacred city of Islam.

Extend: Label the verbs you underlined in the last paragraph as *action* or *linking*.

Auxiliary (Helping) Verbs

Auxiliary (helping) verbs include all the forms of *have, do, be, can, may, shall,* and *will.* (The verbs *have, do,* and *be*—in all of their forms—can also be used as main verbs.) Turn to 714.2 in *Write Source* for a list of auxiliary verbs.

> **Underline** only the auxiliary verbs in the following sentences. You will find 21 words functioning as helping verbs.

1. Jocko the clown <u>has</u> <u>been</u> telling jokes all day.

2. Amiri was exposed to mumps.

3. Francine, can you finish your homework before supper?

4. Wise people will vote for the candidate with the best qualifications.

5. Mosha does not like potato soup.

6. Many cities have provided shelters for the homeless.

7. Should the flight be here by now?

8. The bald eagle will soon be removed from the endangered species list.

9. Oh, the bald eagle has already been removed.

10. Maybe we should celebrate!

11. I have always known that I am a good thinker.

12. The doctor said my stepfather should swim every day.

13. Has your little sister finished her homework?

14. Tomeka, may I join your group?

15. I do like to do yoga twice a week.

16. Yoga does improve my flexibility.

17. It has also helped me feel more centered and calm.

18. We will have been playing cards for almost four hours.

Extend: Choose five helping verbs from the list at 714.2. Write sentences using your verbs as auxiliary verbs, not as main verbs. (Use a form of the verbs *have* and *do* at least once.)

Linking Verbs

Linking verbs (*be, am, is, are, sound, taste*) join subjects to words that rename (predicate noun) or describe (predicate adjective) the subjects. Turn to 714.1 in *Write Source* for a list of linking verbs. (Also see 702.3 and 728.1 for information about predicate nouns and adjectives.)

> **My grandma's spaghetti is my favorite food.** (The linking verb *is* connects the subject *spaghetti* with *food,* a predicate noun that renames the subject.)

> **Wow, that spaghetti tasted great!** (The linking verb *tasted* connects the subject *spaghetti* with *great,* a predicate adjective that describes the subject.)

Complete the following sentences by adding a linking verb and either a predicate noun or a predicate adjective. Circle the linking verbs.

---

1. *(predicate noun)*

The new train ___(is) a monorail.___

2. *(predicate adjective)*

Our old football uniforms _____

3. *(predicate noun)*

The magic show _____

4. *(predicate noun)*

Malcolm's new telephone _____

5. *(predicate noun)*

Emily's new computer _____

6. *(predicate adjective)*

Brody's twice-baked potatoes _____

7. *(predicate adjective)*

This wool shirt _____

8. *(predicate adjective)*

The movie we saw last night _____

Extend: Write five sentences about food. Use a linking verb and colorful predicate nouns and adjectives. (Turn to page 714 in *Write Source*.)

Present Tense Verbs & Third-Person Pronouns

The form of most verbs changes only when a third-person singular pronoun is used with a verb in the present tense. (See the chart below.) Turn to page 718.2 in *Write Source*.

Person	Present Tense	
	Singular	**Plural**
1st person	I learn.	We learn.
2nd person	You learn.	You learn.
3rd person	He, She, It *learns*.	They learn.

> **Write** sentences using the present tense verbs listed below; use pronouns as subjects. (The person and number are indicated for each pronoun.) Then rewrite each sentence using a third-person singular pronoun. Remember to adjust the verb.

1. *go*—(a) first person, plural; (b) third person, singular

   a. We go to the beach every summer.

   b. He goes to the beach every summer.

2. *swim*—(a) third person, plural; (b) third person, singular

   a. _____

   b. _____

3. *enjoy*—(a) first person, singular; (b) third person, singular

   a. _____

   b. _____

4. *ski*—(a) second person, singular; (b) third person, singular

   a. _____

   b. _____

5. *repair*—(a) first person, singular; (b) third person, singular

   a. _____

   b. _____

Extend: Write six sentences using the present tense of the verb *find*. In the first three sentences, use singular first-, second-, and third-person pronouns. In the other three, use plural forms of the three persons of a pronoun.

Active & Passive Voice

The voice of a verb determines if the subject is acting or being acted upon. Writing is generally most effective in the active voice. It's also important to avoid switching between active and passive voice in the same sentence. (Turn to 716.1 and 722.2 and the chart at the bottom of page 722 in *Write Source* for more information.)

> **Earthquakes damage a tremendous amount of property.**
> (*Damage* is an active verb; the subject, *earthquakes,* is doing the acting.)

> **A tremendous amount of property is damaged by earthquakes.**
> (*Is damaged* is a passive verb; the subject, *a tremendous amount of property,* is being acted upon.)

Rewrite the following passive sentences so that they are active.

1. Most earthquakes are generated by shifting plates in the earth's outer shell.

   Shifting plates in the earth's outer shell generate most

   earthquakes.

2. An earthquake's strength is measured with seismographs.

_____

3. Seismic waves that can travel for miles are created by an earthquake.

_____

4. Landslides, fires, and floods can also be caused by earthquakes.

_____

5. Most deaths are caused by collapsing buildings.

_____

6. Tsunamis, enormous ocean waves, are produced by earthquakes beneath the ocean floor.

_____

_____

Extend: Write a paragraph describing a recent event you experienced—a dance, a concert, a ball game, or some other activity. Use active voice in your description.

Present, Past, & Future Verb Tenses

Tense indicates time. The three simple tenses of a verb are present *(I eat)*, past *(I ate)*, and future *(I will eat)*. Turn to 718.4 in *Write Source* for further explanation.

Rewrite each sentence below, changing the verb to the tense indicated.

1. Learning to drive causes me much anxiety.

    Past: _Learning to drive caused me much anxiety._

    Future: _Learning to drive will cause me much anxiety._

2. Mr. Lonetree carves wooden whistles.

    Past: _____

    Future: _____

3. High winds whipped the sea into a sailor's nightmare.

    Future: _____

    Present: _____

4. The football players will take ballet classes.

    Past: _____

    Present: _____

5. New teachers needed knowledge and patience to succeed.

    Present: _____

    Future: _____

6. Rappelling will require strength and courage.

    Past: _____

    Present: _____

Extend: Turn to page 316 in *Write Source*. The first paragraph in the student essay is written in the past tense. Rewrite it first in the present tense and then in the future tense. Note the changes you need to make to each verb to alter its tense.

Perfect Tense Verbs

The three perfect tenses are present perfect (*I have eaten*), past perfect (*I had eaten*), and future perfect (*I will have eaten*). Turn to page 720 in *Write Source* for more information.

> **Form** the perfect tense for each sentence below using the past participle of the verb in parentheses.

1. Many people _____ *have called* _____ Italy's Leaning Tower of Pisa one of the most interesting destinations in Europe. (*call:* present perfect)

2. Depending on how you calculate it, the Leaning Tower _____ for 650 to 800 years. (*exist:* present perfect)

3. Built on sandy soil, it began to sink unevenly after workers _____ the first three stories. (*complete:* past perfect)

4. By the end of the sixteenth century, the Leaning Tower _____ famous for Galileo's experiment on the effects of gravity. (*become:* past perfect)

5. Over the years, engineers _____ many schemes to stop the tower from sinking and leaning. (*try:* present perfect)

6. Until 1991, visitors _____ to climb the 294 steps to the top. (*permit:* past perfect)

7. Engineers _____ an entirely new concrete base for the tower. (*pour:* past perfect)

8. Since the plan worked, these scientists _____ one of the oldest and most famous landmarks of Italy. (*save:* present perfect)

9. If you visit Italy without seeing the Leaning Tower, you _____ seeing a unique structure. (*miss:* future perfect)

Extend: Write three sentences about a tourist attraction you've seen or heard about. Use each of the three perfect verb tenses.

Review: Verbs 1

> **Write** sentences that demonstrate your knowledge of verbs. Use verbs that meet all the requirements listed for each sentence.

1. action verb, present tense, active voice *The weather forecaster predicts sunshine today.*

2. linking verb and predicate adjectives _____

_____

3. linking verb and predicate noun _____

_____

4. action verb, passive voice _____

_____

5. action verb, active voice _____

_____

6. action verb, present perfect tense _____

_____

7. action verb, future perfect tense _____

_____

8. action verb, past perfect tense _____

_____

9. linking verb and predicate adjective _____

_____

10. action verb, past tense, passive voice _____

_____

Transitive & Intransitive Verbs

A transitive verb shows action and is always followed by an object that receives the action. An intransitive verb refers to an action that is complete in itself. It does not need an object to receive the action. (Turn to 716.1 in *Write Source*.) Note that some verbs can be either transitive or intransitive, as in the following examples.

> **Raphael painted the *Alba Madonna*, the *Sistine Madonna*, the *Madonna of the Chair*, and the *Transfiguration*.** (The transitive verb *painted* is followed by multiple direct objects—*Alba Madonna, Sistine Madonna,* and so on.)

> **Raphael Sanzio painted for a living.** (The intransitive verb *painted* expresses a complete action.)

Write a *T* in the blank if the underlined verb is transitive; write an *I* if it is intransitive.

_____*T*_____ **1.** Raphael, one of the great Renaissance painters, <u>influenced</u> artists as late as the early 1900s.

_____ **2.** He <u>painted</u> altarpieces, frescoes (paintings on damp plaster), and portraits.

_____ **3.** Raphael <u>was asked</u> by Pope Julius II to paint the Vatican Palace.

_____ **4.** At the Vatican Palace, Raphael <u>worked</u> with Michelangelo, another great artist.

_____ **5.** Raphael <u>painted</u> an entire ceiling with stories of Cupid and Psyche.

_____ **6.** During this time, Raphael <u>created</u> many religious works, a common subject for painters of this period.

_____ **7.** He traveled to many different countries and <u>learned</u> from the master artists along the way.

_____ **8.** By 1516, Raphael <u>had painted</u> 10 large watercolors of the Apostles.

_____ **9.** Raphael <u>died</u> in Rome at the age of 37.

_____ **10.** Today, his works <u>appear</u> in museums all over the world.

Extend: Write five sentences in which you use transitive verbs. Explain why each verb is transitive.

Direct & Indirect Objects

Transitive verbs always take direct objects (and sometimes indirect objects). Intransitive verbs take neither. Turn to 716.1 and 716.2 in *Write Source* for more information. (Remember that a verb must first have a direct object before it can take an indirect object.)

> **Lora took the candy.**
> (The transitive verb *took* has a direct object, *candy.*)

> **Tyler gave me the candy.**
> (The transitive verb *gave* has a direct object, *candy,* and an indirect object, *me.*)

Direct Object: *candy*	**Indirect Object:** *me*
(Tyler gave *what?*) *candy*	(Tyler gave candy *to whom?*) *me*

> **The candy melted.** (The intransitive verb *melted* has no objects.)

Create sentences using the patterns indicated. You may add modifiers to make your sentences interesting. Finally, answer questions 7 and 8.

1. *(subject + verb + direct object)*

   The horse kicked the gate.

2. *(subject + verb)*

   The gate swung open.

3. *(subject + verb + indirect object + direct object)*

   The opened gate gave the horse a morning's freedom.

4. *(subject + verb + direct object)*

   _____

5. *(subject + verb)*

   _____

6. *(subject + verb + indirect object + direct object)*

   _____

7. Which sentences have transitive verbs? _____

8. Which sentences have intransitive verbs? _____

Writers INC 539.3 and 540.1

Verbals: Gerunds, Infinitives, & Participles

Gerunds, infinitives, and participles are verbals. A verbal is derived from a verb, has the power of a verb, but acts as another part of speech. Turn to 726.1–726.3 in *Write Source*.

Type of Verbal	Functions as		
	Noun	**Adjective**	**Adverb**
gerund (ends in *-ing*)	X		
infinitive (introduced by *to*)	X	X	X
participle (ends in *-ing* or *-ed*)		X	

Underline the verbals in each of the sentences below. Write **G** above each gerund, **I** above each infinitive, and **P** above each participle.

G
1. <u>Talking</u> to my sister gives me energy.

2. I think we need to talk.

3. The woman talking on the phone is my teacher.

4. Mr. Ramirez thanked us for delivering his package.

5. The boy kicking the ball needs to pass it to his teammate.

6. Ulla is about to kick a penalty shot that could win the game.

7. I have an essay to finish tonight.

8. Pushing the car out of the mud was impossible.

9. The young campers, exhausted and sweaty, jumped into the stream.

10. This pile of washed clothes needs to be sorted.

11. Do I have to fold all the laundry?

12. I plan on washing the car before going to the game.

13. The stack of completed reports on the desk is going to fall over soon.

14. Writing causes my hand to cramp up.

15. I was tempted to eat all the ripened strawberries.

Extend: Write three sentences, each using one of the three kinds of verbals for the word *run*.

Irregular Verbs 1

Regular verbs form the past tense and past participle with an *-ed* ending. Irregular verbs form their past tense and past participle in other ways. Turn to the chart on page 720.2 in *Write Source* for examples. (Always use a dictionary if you are unsure of a verb's principal parts.)

Change the irregular verbs in the sentences below from present to past tense.

drove
1. Sensing his opportunity, the golfer ~~drives~~ the ball more than 300 yards down the fairway.

2. He writes a note to himself.

3. Unable to conceal his excitement, he literally runs to the spot where the ball lies.

4. The location for his next shot is perfect.

5. His swift shot with a nine iron does the job, leaving him with a simple putt that gives him the lead.

6. Now he knows victory is at hand as he throws the ball to his caddy standing near the edge of the green.

7. His closest opponent, James, takes a drink of water before trying to complete this final round.

8. James, hoping to delay his putt as long as possible, speaks to someone in the front row of the crowd.

9. James catches the side of the ball with the putter, and the ball breaks badly to the left of the cup.

10. He slowly shakes his head and then graciously goes over to congratulate the winner.

Extend: Write a sentence using the past tense or past participle of each of the following verbs: *shrink, grow, ride, swim, flee,* and *wear.*

Irregular Verbs 2

Regular verbs form the past tense and past participle with an -ed ending. Irregular verbs form their past tense and past participle in other ways. Turn to the chart on page 720.2 in *Write Source* for examples. (Always use a dictionary if you are unsure of a verb's principal parts.)

Use the past participles of the irregular verbs listed below to fill in the blanks in the story. Choose the verb that best fits each sentence. Use each verb only once.

bite, choose, come, creep, drag, fall, feel, find, grow, sit, see, spring, speak, teach, write

1. Just as he feared, the great oak tree had ____*fallen*____ on his neighbor's garage.

2. Josie decided to stay home because she had already _____ that movie.

3. Have you _____ which shirt you are going to wear to the dance?

4. Some tiny creature, perhaps a mouse, had _____ into the box.

5. The grasshopper had mistakenly _____ from the tall grass into the pond.

6. Leon had _____ bad about missing his uncle's impromptu visit.

7. Thanks to his workouts, Jason had _____ strong enough to take on the more challenging ski runs.

8. Greg knew the time had _____ to trade his football gear for a basketball uniform.

9. Lance was surprised that his own dog had _____ him.

10. The boys had _____ the heavy box through the mud onto dry ground.

11. The rusty bucket had _____ outside for several years.

12. Mom asked me if I had _____ my history paper yet.

13. Because Tamisha had _____ the missing pieces, we finished the puzzle.

14. Mr. Grayson realized he had _____ more than 4,000 students in 30 years.

15. After Jeremy had _____ about his Habitat for Humanity experiences, several students wanted to help with the next project in the community.

Extend: Write three to five sentences using irregular verbs to describe a scary situation. First write in the present tense. Then rewrite the sentences in the past perfect tense. Which description sounds more effective?

Verb Moods

The mood of a verb indicates the tone or attitude with which a statement is made. The *indicative mood* is used to state a fact or to ask a question. The *imperative mood* is used to give a command. The *subjunctive mood* is used to express a condition contrary to fact or an unreal condition. Turn to 724.1 in *Write Source* for more information.

> **Can frogs *breathe* underwater? No, but tadpoles *can breathe* underwater.**
> (The indicative mood is used to ask a question or state a fact.)

> **Go to your room immediately!**
> (The imperative mood is used for a command.)

> **If I *were* foolish, I'd never do my homework.**
> (The subjunctive mood is used to express a condition contrary to fact.)

Write a sentence that contains a verb in the mood asked for in each instance below.

1. indicative mood (statement)

Niihau is one of the lesser-known Hawaiian islands.

2. imperative mood

3. subjunctive mood to express a condition contrary to fact

4. imperative mood

5. indicative mood (question)

6. subjunctive mood with *as though* or *as if* to express an unreal condition

7. indicative mood (question)

8. indicative mood (statement—answer the question in number 7)

Review: Verbs 2

Write sentences that follow the patterns listed below. Add other words as needed.

1. *(gerund + transitive verb + indirect object + direct object)*

  Running gave me leg cramps.

2. *(subject + linking verb + predicate adjective)*

_____

3. *(subject + participle + transitive verb + direct object)*

_____

_____

4. *(subject + auxiliary verb + main verb + adverb)*

_____

_____

5. *(subject + transitive verb + indirect object + direct object)*

_____

_____

6. *(subject + verb + infinitive)*

_____

_____

7. *(imperative mood: transitive verb + direct object)*

_____

_____

8. *(subject + linking verb + predicate noun)*

_____

_____

Pretest: Adjectives & Adverbs

Insert an effective adjective or adverb in the sentences below. Identify your choice by writing **ADJ** (adjective) or **ADV** (adverb) on the blank.

ADJ   **1.** India is one of the _____oldest_____ civilizations in the world.

_____   **2.** Sometime between the summer of 1999 and the spring of 2000, India's _____ population exceeded 1 billion.

_____   **3.** India's population has _____ doubled in the last 30 years.

_____   **4.** Some Indians see reaching the 1-billion-people mark as cause for _____ celebration.

_____   **5.** "Nothing is _____ when 1 billion Indians work together!" exclaimed government-sponsored ads in newspapers.

_____   **6.** "We shall overcome everything that stands between today's India and her _____ place among the great nations of the world."

_____   **7.** Only China's population is _____ than India's.

_____   **8.** However, China's growth rate has been _____ than India's in recent years.

_____   **9.** Concerns about population growth have increased _____ during the past several decades.

_____   **10.** This concern is _____ due to the extra demands that the additional population places on human and natural resources.

_____   **11.** Supplies of water, fuel, and food are all _____ strained by huge populations.

_____   **12.** Though some of India's leaders remain confident that India can manage its huge population, others are _____ worried.

Types of Adjectives

An adjective describes a noun or a pronoun. The articles *(a, an, the)* are also adjectives. Turn to 728.1 in *Write Source* for information and examples.

> **Circle** the word in each of the following groups that would *most likely* be used as an adjective. In the blank, indicate whether it is a *common* adjective, a *proper* adjective, or an *article*. Finally, write a sentence using the adjective.

1. through, monkey, (bland,) cook _____*common*_____

   Grandpa must eat bland food to keep his ulcer under control.

2. very, brain, an, disc, sprint _____

   _____

3. shy, trunk, doctor, remain, into _____

   _____

4. Tom, Germany, spot, Wisconsin, Hawaiian _____

   _____

5. rhumba, wacky, newspaper, accident, novel _____

   _____

6. all, bread, skid, Texas, lock _____

   _____

7. book, since, the, sticker, electricity _____

   _____

8. jump, Florida, pen, really, Japanese _____

   _____

Extend: Go back to each of the word groups above and find a different word that could work as an adjective. For example, in the first word group, *monkey* (which is usually a noun) is used as an adjective in the following sentence: *Some people think bananas are monkey food.* Your challenge is to select such a word in each group and use it as an adjective in a sentence.

Forms of Adjectives to Compare

Different forms of adjectives (positive, comparative, and superlative) are used to describe and compare nouns. Turn to 728.2 in *Write Source* for information and examples.

Fill in the blanks with the correct form of each adjective.

	Positive	Comparative	Superlative
1.	cold	*colder*	*coldest*
2.		lower	
3.	late		
4.		more beautiful	
5.		happier	
6.		less likely	
7.	much		

Identify the underlined adjective in each sentence below. Use **P** for positive, **C** for comparative, and **S** for superlative.

_____P_____ **1.** Isaac Asimov is an enormously <u>popular</u> author of both fiction and nonfiction.

_____ **2.** Readers of science fiction think that Asimov's novels are <u>better</u> than those of other authors.

_____ **3.** His fans find his science fiction <u>more interesting</u> than that of other writers.

_____ **4.** On topics ranging from astronomy to limericks, Asimov's books are some of the <u>best</u> books ever written.

_____ **5.** When he died in 1992, the world lost one of the <u>most prolific</u> sci-fi writers who ever lived.

Extend: The following adjectives are irregular and their forms must be memorized: *good, better, best* and *bad, worse, worst.* Use each of these adjectives in a sentence.

Writers INC 545.2

Review: Adjectives

Label the type (common, proper, article) of the underlined adjectives below.

common
1   <u>Many</u> people say that you can't compare apples and oranges. Why not?

2   Apples and oranges are both <u>round</u> fruits that grow on <u>leafy</u> trees. Apple trees

3   belong to <u>the</u> Rosaceae family, and oranges are from the <u>Rutaceae</u> family. Why,

4   they're practically related!

5   <u>Orange</u> trees are evergreens that grow about <u>eight</u> feet tall. Apple trees

6   are <u>taller</u>, unless they are dwarf trees. Fruit trees are among the <u>hardest</u> of

7   all the trees to grow. They need <u>more</u> care than other trees need. <u>United</u>

8   <u>States</u> growers produce about 10 million <u>metric</u> tons of juicy oranges each year

9   and almost as many tons of apples. But apples are <u>the</u> most popular fruit of all

10 in <u>this</u> country.

Label the form (positive, comparative, superlative) of the underlined adjectives below.

1   Apple trees are grown in all 50 states but do better in <u>colder</u> places

2   where the temperature may drop below freezing for several months. The

3   <u>most productive</u> apple-growing states are Washington, New York, Michigan,

4   California, Pennsylvania, and Virginia. There are <u>many</u> varieties of apples. The

5   Delicious apple is one of the <u>more popular</u> apples in the United States.

6   Oranges do not like the cold and only grow where it is <u>warm</u>. The <u>best</u>

7   states of all the orange-growing states are Florida, California, Texas, and

8   Arizona. There are three types of oranges: sweet, <u>sour</u>, and mandarin oranges.

9   The navel orange is the <u>sweetest</u> orange in the Western states.

Types of Adverbs 1

Adverbs modify verbs, adjectives, or other adverbs by telling *how, when, where, how often,* and *how much.* Turn to 730.1 in *Write Source* for information and more examples.

> **Underline** the adverbs in the following paragraphs and label them *how, when, where, how often,* or *how much.* (*Note:* **Do not underline prepositional phrases used as adverbs unless your teacher directs you to do so.**)

            how often   *how much*

1   Oftentimes people do not realize that their activities, hobbies, and interests

2   are preparing them for a particular future. For example, it seems unlikely that

3   T. E. Lawrence, born in Wales in 1888, knew he was preparing for his future

4   when he spent much of his childhood happily exploring castles. It's also unlikely

5   that he knew his trek across the Middle East while in college would later

6   contribute significantly to his career.

7   When World War I began, Lawrence willingly joined the British Army.

8   Later, he was quietly sent on a diplomatic mission into the heart of Arabia to

9   meet warring tribesmen who lived there. Lawrence eventually convinced the

10   tribes to work together. He became passionately devoted to the Arab cause.

11   Next, he helped to organize the Arab revolt against the Turkish Ottoman

12   Empire.

13   After the war, Lawrence wrote his now famous autobiography, *The Seven*

14   *Pillars of Wisdom.* Shortly after retiring from the army in 1935, he tragically

15   died in a motorcycle accident.

16   Lawrence was not famous until Hollywood produced the movie *Lawrence*

17   *of Arabia* in the 1960s. Now many social studies and literature classes view

18   this movie to learn about Arabia, the Turkish Ottoman Empire, and the war

19   between them.

Extend: Write five sentences about another country, using at least one adverb in each sentence. Underline the adverbs and label them *how, when, where, how often,* or *how much.*

          Writers INC 546.1

Types of Adverbs 2

Adverbs modify a verb (or verbal), an adjective, or another adverb. Turn to page 730.1 in *Write Source* for further explanation.

> **Fill in** each blank with an adverb that tells *how, when, where, how often,* or *how much,* as asked for in parentheses. Don't use any adverb more than once.

1. Where I live, we ___*frequently*___ *(how often)* have blizzards.

2. Streets, sidewalks, and cars get _____ *(how much)* buried in snow.

3. _____ *(when)* my sister and I had to go _____ *(where)*

   and shovel the driveway.

4. I _____ *(how)* made a snowball and threw it at my sister.

5. While I built a snowman, she _____ *(how)* made a snowball.

6. My sister _____ *(how often)* aims _____ *(how)*.

7. Just as I put my scarf on the snowman, the sloppy snowball whopped me

   _____ *(how)* between the shoulder blades.

8. Running _____ *(where or how)* was my sister's best defense.

9. I chased her inside, where my dad had been _____ *(how)* making a

   pot of chili.

10. I _____ *(how)* forgot about getting even with her.

11. After lunch, I _____ *(how)* called my friends to go sledding.

12. We met _____ *(when)* to go sledding in Whitnall Park.

13. Our sleds sped _____ *(how)* down the hills.

14. The hills were _____ *(how much)* steep.

15. _____ *(when)* we went home and warmed up with hot chocolate.

Extend: Use the sentences above as models for your own story. Choose adverbs to answer the questions (*how, how much, how often, where,* and *when*) as noted.

Forms of Adverbs

Adverbs, like adjectives, have three forms: *positive, comparative,* and *superlative.* (Turn to 730.2 in *Write Source.*) Use the comparative form to compare two things, the superlative to compare three or more. Most one-syllable adverbs take the endings *-er* or *-est* (*soon, sooner, soonest*) to create the comparative and superlative forms; but longer adverbs and almost all those ending in *-ly* use *more* and *most* or *less* and *least* (*more ambitiously, most ambitiously; less ambitiously, least ambitiously*).

Use each of the following adverbs in a sentence. Use the form listed in parentheses.

1. often (comparative)

    Does Lori come here more often than John?

2. close (positive)

3. early (superlative)

4. occasionally (positive)

5. well (comparative)

6. smoothly (superlative)

7. swiftly (comparative)

8. slowly (superlative)

Extend: Choose two adverbs, one that uses *-er* or *-est* and one that uses *less* or *least,* to form comparisons. Write sentences using each adverb in the three forms: positive, comparative, and superlative.

Review: Adverbs

Underline the adverbs in the following paragraph.

1   <u>Yesterday</u> we received the weekly newscast that we always look forward
2   to. It is really quite decent of Mr. Pepy to bring our supplies and stay to let us
3   listen to the news on his truck's radio. It's not that we love the news—wars,
4   taxes, fires, murders, people acting stupidly in a thousand different ways—no,
5   what we love is the man who delivers the news. We imagine him sitting
6   regally in a fine office—lots of chairs; fancy, electric lights; a very large wooden
7   desk; a swivel chair for himself. He wears a suit (a piece of clothing we've
8   never actually seen) and a necktie. His voice soars across the entire nation,
9   dropping profoundly, rising excitedly, carrying us along on every word. He
10   speaks for only 15 minutes. It is our dream to leave forever the valley where
11   we live so quietly, leave this high range where we tend flocks throughout the
12   summer, to become newscasters.

Write sentences according to the directions given below. Remember that a writer uses adverbs to add detail or color to a sentence.

1. Use an adverb that tells how someone does something.

_____

2. Use *substantially* to tell how much.

_____

3. Use an adverb that tells time: when, how often, or how long.

_____

4. Use an adverb to tell place: where, to where, or from where.

_____

5. Use the comparative form of *quietly*.

_____

6. Use the superlative form of *fast*.

_____

Pretest: Prepositions, Conjunctions, & Interjections

> **Underline** the prepositional phrases in the sentences below and circle the prepositions. Write **O** above the objects of the prepositions.

1. Both eagles and falcons began disappearing (during) the time DDT (a pesticide) was used extensively in this country.

2. By 1975, there were only 325 pairs of nesting peregrine falcons in North America, down from thousands just 30 years earlier.

3. Before that time, eagles and falcons were seen in abundance, nesting on river bluffs.

4. Although peregrine falcons are the swiftest birds on earth, speed is no protection against poison.

> **Underline** the interjections and conjunctions below. Write each one in the appropriate column at the bottom of the page.

1. Well, DDT has been banned throughout the United States for years, and the results with regard to falcons have been dramatic.

2. Because we began protecting the peregrine falcon population, it has been on the rise, so in 1999, there were 1,650 nesting pairs of peregrine falcons.

3. Wow! That's a good argument for conservation, but we can do even better.

4. Either we protect our endangered species, or we will see more of them disappear from our world.

Interjections	Coordinating Conjunctions	Correlative Conjunctions	Subordinating Conjunctions
Well			

Prepositions & Interjections

A prepositional phrase is made up of a preposition and an object (a noun or a pronoun that follows the preposition), plus any words that modify the object. For example, in the phrase "into the river," *into* is the preposition, *river* is the object, and *the* modifies *river*. Turn to pages 732 and 734 in *Write Source* for more information.

> **Underline** each prepositional phrase below, and write **O** above the objects of the prepositions. Label the interjections with an *I*.

                                  O   O   O   O

1. Each state <u>in the union</u> has surface water <u>in the form</u> <u>of lakes</u>, bays, or

    O

<u>streams</u>.

2. Tourists can find more surface water in Rhode Island than in Vermont.

Incredible!

3. In the western part of the country, some of the largest states have very little

water.

4. Travelers enjoy the 40,000 square miles of surface water found in Michigan.

5. Of all the states, Alaska has the largest amount of surface water.

6. Some people enjoy rafting the white-water rivers found throughout our country.

7. Others prefer drifting peacefully on meandering streams.

8. On large lakes, water-skiers fly along pulled behind powerboats.

9. Those who love to fish seek out special spots away from the noise.

10. Although pollution is a problem in many places, there are lakes and streams

that are ideal for swimming. Yippee!

11. Come on! Enjoy the lakes and rivers, but keep garbage out of the water.

Extend: Phrasal prepositions are made up of more than one word: *along with, from among, in addition to, instead of, next to,* and *up to.* Use each of these phrasal prepositions in a sentence. Underline each prepositional phrase. You may write about a celebrity, a hero or heroine, or a topic of your choice.

Coordinating Conjunctions

Study the following examples to learn how to use coordinating conjunctions. Turn to 734.1 and the chart "Kinds of Conjunctions" in *Write Source* for more examples and an explanation.

> **Kayaking can be a fun *and* exciting sport.**
> (The coordinating conjunction *and* connects two equal words.)

> **A good kayak should glide swiftly *yet* turn easily.**
> (The coordinating conjunction *yet* connects two phrases.)

> **Kayaks are much like canoes, *but* they are enclosed to keep water out.**
> (The coordinating conjunction *but* connects two clauses.)

Combine the sentences below with the coordinating conjunction listed in parentheses.

1. Some kayaks are built out of wood. Other kayaks are made of plastic. Kayaks can also be constructed of fiberglass. *(or)*

Kayaks are built out of wood, plastic, or fiberglass.

2. Kayakers must be skilled with a double-bladed paddle. Kayakers need to make a variety of paddle strokes. *(for)*

_____

_____

3. Kayakers must make forward strokes. Another stroke is the backstroke. Another type of stroke is the sweep stroke. *(and)*

_____

_____

4. One stroke moves the kayak sideways. Another stroke turns the kayak around. *(and)*

_____

_____

5. One of the most popular kayaking strokes is the Eskimo roll. This stroke is one of the most difficult to master. *(yet)*

_____

_____

Extend: Write sentences about an activity that you enjoy. Try to use all seven coordinating conjunctions listed in the chart on page 734.

Correlative Conjunctions

Study the examples below to see how to use correlative conjunctions. Turn to 734.2 and the chart "Kinds of Conjunctions" in *Write Source* for more examples and an explanation.

> **Mountain biking is *both* exciting *and* dangerous.** (The correlative conjunctions *both* and *and* connect two equal words.)

> **Mountain bikes are used *either* on streets *or* on dirt trails.** (The correlative conjunctions *either* and *or* connect two equal phrases.)

> ***Whether* you ride to school *or* you compete in a race, mountain bikes are fun.** (The correlative conjunctions *whether* and *or* connect two equal clauses.)

Combine the sentences below using the correlative conjunctions listed in parentheses.

1. The list of biker safety equipment includes a helmet. Reflectors are important, too. *(not only, but also)*

The list of biker safety equipment includes not only a helmet but

also reflectors.

2. You need strength to climb hills. You also need endurance. *(both, and)*

3. Usually, street curbs don't stop a mountain biker. Also, fallen branches don't stop a mountain biker. *(neither, nor)*

4. When biking in the country, always have a spare tire. This is also true for traveling in the city. *(whether, or)*

5. Touring in the backcountry is a great way to bike. It includes all the adventure of camping. *(not only, but also)*

Extend: Write five sentences using the five pairs of correlative conjunctions listed in the chart on page 734 in *Write Source*. You can write about camping, biking, or whatever other activity you like. Make your sentences pertain to one subject so you can write them as a paragraph.

Subordinating Conjunctions

Study the example below to review how a subordinating conjunction connects an independent clause to a dependent clause. Turn to 734.3 and the chart "Kinds of Conjunctions" in *Write Source* for more information.

> **We hiked all day although it was raining.** (The clause *although it was raining* is dependent. It depends on the rest of the sentence to complete its meaning.)

Complete the following sentences with a dependent clause that begins with the underlined subordinating conjunction.

1. She will not go swimming <u>because</u> *she is afraid of water.*

2. We wouldn't be surprised to find out <u>that</u> _____

_____

3. The waiter did not come back to our table <u>until</u> _____

_____

4. <u>Since</u> _____

_____ we seldom go to the movies.

5. He can sing at the prom <u>as long as</u> _____

_____

6. <u>If</u> _____

_____ my favorite wrestler would have won the cage match.

7. Detectives sit in their car and eat <u>while</u> _____

_____

8. Mrs. Sell, the librarian, charged Sam $20 <u>after</u> _____

_____

9. I like growing up in a large city <u>where</u> _____

_____

Extend: Choose one of the sentences above and write a paragraph based on that sentence. Include at least two sentences that connect an independent and a dependent clause with a subordinating conjunction.

     Writers INC 548.3

Review: Prepositions, Conjunctions, & Interjections

Underline each prepositional phrase. Then label each interjection in the sentences below with an **I** and each conjunction with a **C**.

1. *I* — *C*
   Wow, I just finished reading *The Complete Sherlock Holmes,* and I discovered a lot of facts I never knew about Holmes.

2. Not only was Holmes extremely moody, but he also had some very weird habits.

3. He would get depressed and lie around for days, scraping away on his violin and driving Dr. Watson nearly over the edge.

4. Although he could play the violin brilliantly when he wished, Sherlock simply screeched out of tune during his depressions.

5. When Holmes wanted to smoke his pipe, he had to get his tobacco from the place where he stashed it—in the toe of his Persian slippers.

6. He also kept his mail in order in an unusual way; Holmes stuck it safely to the mantelpiece with his pocketknife.

7. Holmes had an older brother named Mycroft Holmes who appeared in three stories.

8. Well, Sherlock was brilliant, but Mycroft was brilliant beyond belief.

9. Because Mycroft had no ambition, he left his room only on rare occasions and then only for a brief time.

10. Both Sherlock and Mycroft were well above average in intelligence, but they were also on the eccentric side.

Review: Parts of Speech Activities

Complete the following statements.

1. A noun or a pronoun is in the objective case when it is used as a direct object, a/an ___*indirect object*___ , or a/an _____ .

2. A/An _____ shows strong emotion or surprise.

3. A/An _____ can be used in place of a noun.

4. Both nouns and pronouns have three cases: _____ , objective, and _____ .

5. *Who, whose, whom, which,* and *that* are relative _____ .

6. The _____ form of adjectives and adverbs compares two persons, places, things, or ideas.

7. A/An _____ expresses action or state of being.

8. *I see* is an example of _____ tense.

9. In the sentence *Renaldo showed me his skateboard yesterday,* the word _____ is the direct object.

10. A gerund is a/an _____ form that ends in *-ing* and is used as a noun.

11. An infinitive is usually introduced by the word _____ .

12. A/An _____ pronoun relates an adjective clause to the noun or pronoun it modifies.

13. Adverbs modify _____ , _____ , or _____ .

14. A/An _____ is a word that names a person, a place, a thing, or an idea.

15. In the sentence *Tarzan is smart,* the word *smart* is a predicate _____ .

16. The _____ form of adjectives compares three or more persons, places, things, or ideas.

17. In the sentence *David was snoozing,* the word *was* is a/an _____

verb.

18. When a noun or a pronoun shows ownership, it is in the _____

case.

19. In the phrase *behind the door,* the word *behind* is a/an _____ .

20. *And, but, or, for, nor, yet,* and *so* are coordinating _____ .

21. A/An _____ pronoun points out people, places, or things without

naming them.

22. *Since* is a/an _____ conjunction.

23. A/An _____ noun names a particular person, place, thing, or idea.

24. *I saw* is an example of _____ tense.

25. A/An _____ noun names a group or a unit.

26. The pronoun *our* is in the _____ person.

27. Adjectives describe or modify _____ or _____ .

28. *Who* is a/an _____ or a/an _____ pronoun.

29. In the sentence *Britt gave me a birthday present,* the word *me* is a/an

_____ .

30. A/An _____ connects individual words or groups of words.

31. A/An _____ or a/an _____ is most often used as

the subject of a sentence, but a gerund or an infinitive may also be used.

32. In the sentence *I admire her persistence,* the verb is in the _____

voice.

33. The _____ person is used to name the person or thing spoken about.

34. Many adverbs end in _____ .

35. *Both/and* and *not only/but also* are _____ conjunctions.

Sentence Activities

The activities in this section cover three important areas: (1) the basic parts, types, and kinds of sentences as well as agreement issues; (2) methods for writing smooth-reading sentences; and (3) common sentence errors. Most activities include practice in which you review, combine, or analyze different sentences. In addition, the **Extend** activities provide follow-up practice with certain skills.

Sentence Basics   123

Sentence Combining   153

Sentence Problems   159

Sentence Review   183

Pretest: Subjects & Predicates

> **Draw** a line between the complete subject and the complete predicate in each sentence. Then underline the simple or compound subject once and the simple or compound predicate twice.

1. Athletes | hit the ball, leap the hurdle, and go the distance.

2. People of all ages and abilities love sports.

3. More than 1 million athletes, representing 150 countries as well as all 50 American states, participate in the Special Olympics.

4. The athletes who compete in the Special Olympics are both like and unlike other athletes.

5. Like all Olympic contestants, Special Olympians enjoy the thrill of competition and appreciate the special camaraderie of the games.

6. They train hard to do their best.

7. Each Special Olympian has some degree of mental retardation.

8. That single fact does not prevent a Special Olympian from enjoying sports, however.

9. The public and the media often overlook the heroic accomplishments of Special Olympians.

10. But these athletes understand the joy of sports.

11. Winning is important.

12. Bravery, determination, persistence, and good sportsmanship count for even more.

Subjects & Predicates 1

A *sentence* must have a subject and a predicate that together express a complete thought. A *simple subject* is the subject without its modifiers; a *simple predicate* is the verb without its modifiers. *Complete subjects* and *complete predicates* contain all the modifiers, too. Turn to 738.1–740.1 in *Write Source* for information and examples.

> **Draw** a line between the complete subject and the complete predicate. Underline each simple subject once and each simple predicate twice.

1. A <u>flock</u> of turkey vultures | <u>landed</u> in a pasture across the road yesterday.

2. Tariq wondered why they had landed there.

3. Carrion—the decaying flesh of dead animals—is the main source of food for vultures.

4. Looking around the pasture, Tariq saw no dead animals.

5. These big, ugly birds of prey were perhaps hunting for a safe place to rest.

6. Turkey vultures are related to birds even bigger and uglier than they are.

7. For instance, vultures living in the mountains of the Mediterranean region and in central Asia have a wingspan of about nine feet!

8. Another kind of vulture, the California condor, boasts an equally impressive wingspan of nine to ten feet.

9. The California condor is an endangered species.

10. Scientists began breeding these rare birds in captivity during the 1980s.

11. The condor is slowly making a comeback, thanks to the efforts of scientists and environmentalists.

Extend: Write three or four basic sentences with a simple subject and a simple predicate. Expand the sentences, adding details to both the subject and the predicate.

Subjects & Predicates 2

A *compound subject* is composed of two or more simple subjects. A *compound predicate* is composed of two or more simple predicates. Turn to 738.1–740.1 in *Write Source* for examples.

> **Draw** a line between the complete subject and the complete predicate. Underline any compound subjects or compound predicates.

1. <u>You</u> and <u>I</u> | need to help your grandmother, Michael.

2. The orange ceramic tiger and the blue glass dolphin are missing from her apartment.

3. They have been missing for several days.

4. Your grandmother and her upstairs neighbor are quite fond of those figurines.

5. Grandma received the dolphin from her father and bought the tiger at the 1939 World's Fair in New York.

6. You and I will start looking in her cupboards.

7. Grandma may have cleaned and put away the figurines.

8. I remember she forgot where she put her purse last June.

9. I think you are right. We will find them.

10. You and Sarah can check the guest room.

11. I will go outside and check the garage.

12. "Mom and Grandma, we found the tiger and the dolphin under the sofa!"

13. We examined them carefully and put them back on the shelf.

14. Neither the tiger nor the dolphin is damaged.

15. Grandma and I thank you both for helping.

Extend: Using a friend and yourself as the compound subject, write three to five sentences that include compound predicates.

Review: Subjects & Predicates

Write the correct term for each of the following definitions.

___subject___ **1.** the part of the sentence about which something is said

_____ **2.** must have a subject and a predicate (but either the subject or the predicate may be "understood")

_____ **3.** simple subject and all the words that modify it

_____ **4.** the verb without its modifiers

_____ **5.** one or more words that express a complete thought

_____ **6.** simple predicate and all the words that modify it

_____ **7.** the part of the sentence that shows action or says something about the subject

Draw a line between the complete subject and the complete predicate. Then underline the simple or compound subject once and the simple or compound predicate twice.

1. <u>Maya</u> and her <u>sister</u> | <u>competed</u> against each other in a chess tournament.

2. Hundreds of purple and yellow butterflies darted carelessly through the meadow.

3. The teaching styles of high school teachers are as different as their personalities.

4. The marching band, led by the drummers, increased the pace and cranked up the volume.

5. Neither Red nor I had ever seen or heard such a performance.

Write a sentence with a complete subject and a compound predicate.

_____

_____

Pretest: Phrases

> **Identify** each italicized phrase in the sentences below. On the blanks, write **V** for verbal, **P** for prepositional, or **A** for appositive.

V   **1.** Would you like *to be a Blue Angel*?

_____ **2.** Who hasn't heard *of the Blue Angels*?

_____ **3.** The Blue Angels, *the most famous flight demonstration team in the world*, are Navy and Marine Corps pilots.

_____ **4.** *To fly with speed and precision* is their goal.

_____ **5.** *Being in A-1 physical condition* is a minimum requirement.

_____ **6.** Their bodies, kept physically fit *by vigorous exercise*, must respond perfectly during every flight.

_____ **7.** The pilots say that their 45-minute flight demonstrations require the effort and focus *of an 8-hour day*.

_____ **8.** Their planes, *models equipped with special controls*, fly remarkably close to one another.

_____ **9.** *Flying in tight formation*, the Blue Angels keep their wingtips just 18 to 36 inches apart.

_____ **10.** *To imagine the intensity of the experience,* try holding your muscles contracted for 45 minutes.

_____ **11.** In October 2004, the Blue Angels performed *for 200,000 fascinated spectators* in Jacksonville, Florida.

_____ **12.** Their demonstrations, *precision ballets in the sky,* kept 17 million spectators in awe at 70 air shows in 2004.

Verbal Phrases

Gerunds, infinitives, and participles are verbals. A *verbal* is derived from a verb, has the power of a verb, but acts as another part of speech. Turn to 726.1–726.3 in *Write Source* for examples and more information.

	Functions as		
Type of Verbal	**Noun**	**Adjective**	**Adverb**
gerund (ends in *-ing*)	X		
infinitive (introduced by *to*)	X	X	X
participle (ends in *-ing* or *-ed*)		X	

Identify the underlined verbal phrases in the following sentences. Write **G** for gerund, **I** for infinitive, and **P** for participial.

1. A person must decide whether or not <u>to use slang</u> in everyday situations. *I*

2. <u>Using slang</u> is not always appropriate.

3. A formal paper <u>filled with slang terms</u> makes the writer appear uneducated.

4. The decision <u>to use slang</u> can be the result of a desire <u>to appear cool</u>.

5. Others use slang <u>to put people at ease</u>, <u>to express friendliness</u>, or <u>to be informal</u>.

6. Slang terms <u>expressed in a humorous way</u> can make conversation much more entertaining.

7. People sometimes use slang <u>to refer to painful or frightening events</u>.

8. Before <u>taking a test</u>, a student might use a cliche like "It's time <u>to face the music</u>."

9. Some slang is the result of <u>dropping one or more syllables from a longer word</u>, also called *clipping*.

10. Slang words <u>created in this fashion</u> include *B-Ball*, short for "basketball," and *rep*, short for "reputation" or "representative."

Extend: Develop three to five sentences about the slang you use. Use a different type of verbal phrase in each sentence. Label each of your verbal phrases.

Prepositional & Appositive Phrases

A *prepositional phrase* consists of a preposition, its object, and any modifiers. An *appositive phrase,* which consists of a noun and its modifiers, follows another noun or pronoun and renames it. Turn to the tops of pages 742 and 744 in *Write Source* for examples.

> **Write** an appositive phrase or a prepositional phrase as indicated to complete each sentence below.

1. I decided to go to the concert _____ *in the park* _____ .
prepositional phrase

2. The performers, _____ , seemed to be
appositive phrase
surprised at the size of the crowd.

3. _____ , the emcee had the hiccups.
prepositional phrase

4. _____ , I stopped for a steaming hot cup of coffee.
prepositional phrase

5. I began reading an article _____
prepositional phrase
that someone had left on the table.

6. It was about the members of Graham, _____ .
appositive phrase

7. Sasha Ming, _____ , wrote the article.
appositive phrase

8. A man _____ politely inquired, "May I
prepositional phrase
sit here?"

9. I immediately recognized him as Jeff, _____ .
appositive phrase

10. My brother, _____ , used to date Jeff's sister.
appositive phrase

11. _____ , Jeff and I discovered we had a lot in common.
prepositional phrase

12. Jeff, _____ , was excited about our chance meeting.
appositive phrase

Extend: Write three or four sentences about a concert or musical performers. Include an appositive phrase or a prepositional phrase in each sentence.

Absolute Phrases

An *absolute phrase* consists of a noun and a participle (a word often ending in *-ing* or *-ed*); it acts as an adjective. Absolute phrases can also contain an object and/or modifiers. Study the examples below and turn to the top of page 744 in *Write Source.*

How can you be certain you have composed an absolute phrase? Try adding *was* or *were* to each absolute phrase in the sentences below. If the addition of *was* or *were* makes a complete sentence, you can be certain you have an absolute phrase.

> **The wolves chased the sheep.** (basic sentence)

> **Mouths drooling, eyes shining, the wolves chased the sheep.** (absolute phrases)

> **Mouths drooling like rabid animals, eyes shining in anticipation, the wolves chased the sheep.** (absolute phrases containing modifiers)

Underline the absolute phrases in the following sentences. Next, write sentences using the models as patterns.

---

1. <u>Hands shaking</u>, <u>voice trembling</u>, the actor stepped onto the stage.

   Feet flying, arms flailing, the skater fell.

2. The running back, his legs churning powerfully, slammed into the defensive line.

   _____

   _____

3. The folders fell on the floor, pages scattering in all directions.

   _____

   _____

4. Its numbers dwindling from exhaustion and starvation, Napoleon's defeated army wandered westward.

   _____

   _____

5. The victorious candidate, her supporters cheering loudly, tried to hear the reporters' questions.

   _____

   _____

Extend: Write three or four sentences that contain absolute phrases.

Effective Phrases

Professional writers engage a reader with the skillful use of phrases, adding detail and variety to their sentences. To review the types of phrases, turn to 742.1–744 in *Write Source*.

> **Create** sentences that imitate these examples from well-known works. Circle the phrases you use.

1. *(two gerund phrases)* I like sitting on the side and watching the band play . . .
— Dick Gregory, "Not Poor, Just Broke"

Dad suggested (swimming in the river) and (watching the moon rise.)

2. *(one prepositional phrase and two participial phrases)* The dogs' feet fell heavily on the trail, jarring their bodies and doubling the fatigue of a day's travel.
—Jack London, *The Call of the Wild*

_____

_____

3. *(seven prepositional phrases)* In the corner of the sofa, there was a cushion, and in the velvet which covered it, there was a hole, and out of the hole peeped a tiny head with a pair of frightened eyes in it.
—Frances Hodgson Burnett, *The Secret Garden*

_____

_____

_____

4. *(two infinitive phrases connected with a conjunction)* Bannerman looked as though he didn't know whether to laugh at Johnny or to deal him a good swift kick.
—Stephen King, *The Dead Zone*

_____

_____

5. *(one participial phrase and three prepositional phrases)* The boy, regaining his balance, dragged Sounder off the porch and to the corner of the cabin.
—William H. Armstrong, *Sounder*

_____

_____

Extend: Using one of your sentences as a topic sentence, write a paragraph. Use a variety of phrases in your sentences.

Review: Phrases

Write sentences following the directions given below.

1. Use an appositive phrase and underline it.

_____

_____

_____

2. Use a gerund phrase as a subject and underline it.

_____

_____

3. Use a gerund phrase as the object of a preposition and underline it.

_____

_____

4. Use an infinitive phrase as a subject and underline it.

_____

_____

5. Use prepositional phrases and underline them.

_____

_____

6. Use prepositional phrases and underline them.

_____

_____

7. Use an absolute phrase and underline it.

_____

_____

Pretest: Clauses

> **Identify** each underlined clause, using *I* for independent and *D* for dependent. For each dependent clause, identify it as an adjective clause (*ADJ*), an adverb clause (*ADV*), or a noun clause (*N*).

1. Many eyes in the world focused on the last solar eclipse of the twentieth
century, <u>which occurred on August 11, 1999.</u>
                     D/ADJ

2. Although it was primarily visible in Europe, <u>the 1999 event was one of the most widely seen eclipses in history, thanks to television's coverage.</u>

3. We looked only indirectly at the eclipse, <u>although we were wearing sunglasses.</u>

4. <u>Since looking directly at an eclipse can cause blindness,</u> viewers should shield their eyes properly.

5. <u>A solar eclipse occurs</u> when the moon passes between the sun and the earth, casting a shadow.

6. If the solar eclipse is total, <u>the sun completely disappears from view in some places on earth.</u>

7. Scientists have studied <u>what happens during a solar eclipse.</u>

8. In seconds, day becomes night and temperatures plummet, <u>which is a direct result of the absence of sunlight.</u>

9. <u>In 1999, thousands of Europeans cheered</u> as the moon's shadow fell upon them.

10. <u>Whoever watched from Romania</u> observed the longest period of darkness: 2 minutes and 23 seconds.

11. Few people saw the eclipse on April 8, 2005 <u>because few people live where the eclipse occurred.</u>

12. A solar eclipse is a natural phenomenon <u>that can help scientists learn more about our red-hot power source, the sun.</u>

Independent & Dependent Clauses

A *clause* is a group of related words that has both a subject and a predicate. An *independent clause* can stand alone as a sentence, while a *dependent clause* cannot. Turn to 744.1–744.2 in *Write Source* for examples.

> **Underline** each independent clause once and each dependent clause twice.

1. Bombay, which has a population of more than 16 million, is the largest city in India.

2. Because it is an island city, several bridges link Bombay with the mainland.

3. Most people live in cheap housing in outlying neighborhoods, although wealthy residents occupy modern apartments in the central city.

4. Almost a million people live in dilapidated shanties without proper sanitation, while thousands of others are homeless.

5. Since overcrowding is such a serious problem, the government has been developing a new industrial and residential area on the mainland near Bombay.

6. The principal religion is Hinduism, though Islam has many followers as well.

7. This enormous city, which boasts numerous banks and insurance companies, is a major financial center.

8. Bombay is also a major producer of cotton textiles and leather, which are exported all over the world.

9. Before Bombay became part of India, it was a commerce post founded by Portuguese traders in the 1530s.

10. When King Charles II of England married a Portuguese princess in 1661, he received Bombay as a wedding gift!

Extend: Living in a city of 16 million people must present a number of challenges to everyday life. Write four (or more) sentences describing how you'd overcome these challenges. Include dependent clauses in your sentences.

Adverb, Adjective, & Noun Clauses

There are three types of dependent clauses: *adverb clauses*, beginning with subordinating conjunctions (*when, since, if,* and so on.); *adjective clauses,* beginning with relative pronouns (*who, which, that,* and so on.); and noun clauses, beginning with *what, whatever, that, who,* or *whoever.* (Turn to 744.2 in *Write Source* for further explanation.)

> *Adverb Clause:*
> **My mother took me shopping, because she wanted to cheer me up.**
> (The clause is used as an *adverb* to modify the verb *took*.)

> *Adjective Clause:*
> **She must be thinking I'm like my sister Sarah, who loves to shop.**
> (The clause is used as an *adjective* to modify the noun *Sarah*.)

> *Noun Clause:*
> **Shop until you drop is what Sarah likes to do.**
> (The clause is used as a *noun,* in this case a *predicate noun.*)

Underline the dependent clauses in the following sentences and identify them as **ADV** for adverb, **ADJ** for adjective, or **N** for noun.

1. Half of all people in the United States live in suburbs, <u>while roughly a quarter</u> **ADV**

   <u>of all people in the United States inhabit rural areas.</u>

2. We could see that Althea was not a good swimmer.

3. Some Moroccan musicians who were playing folk melodies in the park will be on

   the TV news tonight.

4. I'll use the parts that I salvaged from the old car to fix the new one.

5. After you sort the laundry, put a load in the washing machine.

6. Whoever plans to go on the field trip should be on the bus at 8:00 a.m. sharp.

7. Yes, you may take the car, as long as you've finished your homework.

8. Eli, whose father is a pilot, travels frequently.

9. What the officer said surprised me.

10. The fact that you like him is no reason to act so silly.

Review: Clauses

Identify each underlined clause, using **D** for dependent and **I** for independent.

1. Viruses, <u>which are microscopic organisms</u> ^D that live inside the cells of other living things, are a major cause of disease.

2. Viruses are <u>primitive particles</u> that only become active inside a living cell.

3. They lack some of the substances <u>that they need for independence</u>, so they enter the cell of a living thing and use the cell's materials to live and reproduce.

4. Most viruses can be seen only with an electron microscope <u>because their size ranges from .01 to .3 microns</u>.

5. <u>Viruses cause disease by damaging the cells of an organism</u>, although a virus sometimes lives in a cell without harming it.

Identify each dependent clause underlined below as **ADJ** for adjective, **ADV** for adverb, and **N** for noun.

1. A cell <u>that is infected by a virus</u> ^{ADJ} produces proteins <u>that the virus needs</u>. ^{ADJ}

2. <u>After the virus uses these proteins</u>, the chemical composition of the cell is changed; as a result, the cell may be damaged or killed.

3. <u>Because the cell proteins are available to the virus</u>, it can reproduce itself hundreds of times.

4. Research has clearly shown <u>that the newly produced viruses leave the cell and infect other cells</u>.

5. Most drugs <u>that are able to kill or damage a virus</u> also damage healthy cells.

6. <u>Because doctors cannot stop a virus from causing disease</u>, they merely attempt to control the symptoms.

Pretest: Sentences

Insert end punctuation in the following sentences. On the first blank, identify each sentence as **S** for simple, **CD** for compound, **CX** for complex, or **CD-CX** for compound-complex. On the second blank, identify each sentence as **D** for declarative, **IN** for interrogative, **IM** for imperative, or **E** for exclamatory.

___S___ ___IN___ **1.** Why is Alfred Hitchcock called the master of suspense?

_____ _____ **2.** If you have to ask that question, you probably haven't seen any of his films, or you haven't thought much about them

_____ _____ **3.** Turn to any list of the greatest movie directors of all time, and you will see Alfred Hitchcock's name near the top

_____ _____ **4.** Have you seen the chilling attack in *The Birds,* when the actress Tippi Hedren fends off murderous gulls, or have you seen the thrilling chase in *North by Northwest,* when Cary Grant tries to outrun a crop duster

_____ _____ **5.** Yikes, I'd almost forgotten that those scenes were so scary

_____ _____ **6.** Have you seen reruns of Hitchcock's weekly TV shows, which he introduced with a dignified walk and a sinister comment

_____ _____ **7.** Audiences found Hitchcock mysterious and entertaining, and they found his movies and TV shows riveting

_____ _____ **8.** The real Alfred Hitchcock was a kind, loyal, sensitive, hardworking man who was devoted to his wife and daughter

_____ _____ **9.** You've got to be kidding

_____ _____ **10.** Truth is stranger than fiction, and everyone admits that Alfred Hitchcock was fond of strangeness

Kinds of Sentences

The four kinds of sentences are declarative, interrogative, imperative, and exclamatory. A sentence might make a statement, ask a question, give a command, or make an exclamation. Turn to 746.1 in *Write Source* for examples.

> **Identify** the following sentences with a *D* for declarative, *IN* for interrogative, *IM* for imperative, or *E* for exclamatory. Add end punctuation.

_____*D*_____ **1.** Last summer, my family drove to the East Coast for a vacation.

_____ **2.** What a disaster it was

_____ **3.** Have you ever sat in a traffic jam for well over an hour

_____ **4.** We did, and then the car's radiator overheated

_____ **5.** We finally got to see the Atlantic Ocean, but it was not what we expected

_____ **6.** Who would have predicted that it would be only 60 degrees in July

_____ **7.** Don't swim in the ocean when it's so chilly on the beach

_____ **8.** Instead, look for seashells

> **Write** four of your own sentences (one of each kind). Don't forget the end punctuation.

1. Declarative: _____

_____

2. Imperative: _____

_____

3. Interrogative: _____

_____

4. Exclamatory: _____

_____

Extend: Write three interrogative sentences on a sheet of paper, leaving room for answers. Exchange with a classmate, and answer the questions using one declarative, one imperative, and one exclamatory sentence.

Types of Sentences 1

The best writing contains a variety of sentence types: *simple, compound, complex,* and *compound-complex.* Practice creating these four types of sentences. Turn to 748.1 in *Write Source.*

> **Write** sentences following the directions given below.

1. Write a simple sentence using this compound subject: *pizza and pineapple.*

Pizza and pineapple are my favorite foods. _____

2. Write a compound sentence. Use the sentence you wrote above and connect it to another sentence with a coordinating conjunction: *and, but, or, for, yet, nor, so.*

_____

_____

_____

3. Write a complex sentence starting with this independent clause: *many people prefer to eat favorite foods.* Add a dependent clause that begins with *that.*

_____

_____

_____

4. Write a compound-complex sentence. (Try to combine the ideas from your second and third sentences.)

_____

_____

_____

5. Write a compound sentence about your neighborhood. Combine the two independent clauses with a semicolon, or with a comma and a coordinating conjunction.

_____

_____

_____

Types of Sentences 2

You can determine the structure of a sentence (*simple, compound, complex,* or *compound-complex*) by looking at the number of dependent and independent clauses. Turn to 748.1 in *Write Source* for more information.

Identify the structure of the following sentences.

_____ *simple* _____ **1.** My family loves to go to restaurants for dinner.

_____ **2.** The word *restaurant* comes from a Latin word meaning *to restore.*

_____ **3.** It makes sense that people need to be "restored" after a long, hard day.

_____ **4.** School and work demand a lot of time; we become exhausted.

_____ **5.** Sometimes we work for hours, and we forget to eat, despite hunger pangs that are trying to tell us something.

_____ **6.** We get comfort and nourishment from food—but it sure makes life easier when someone else makes and serves it.

Write four of your own sentences, using a different structure for each one.

1. Simple: _____

_____

2. Compound: _____

_____

3. Complex: _____

_____

4. Compound-Complex: _____

_____

_____

Extend: Write the first draft of a paragraph. You may describe how you keep your head while living an active life or you may choose another topic. Use a variety of sentence structures.

Sentence Modeling 1

Writers learn how to arrange sentences so they can achieve sentence variety and add details. One way to achieve variety is to put the main clause in different positions—at the beginning, in the middle, or at the end. Turn to 750.1 in *Write Source*.

> **Study** the following sentences. Then write your own version of each sentence, imitating the model part by part. The main clause in each sentence is underlined.

1. <u>Jeremy looked at his friend</u>, shaking his head.

   Janelle stopped at her locker, holding her backpack.

   _____

2. <u>It was almost quarter to six</u> as Jeremy trudged toward his front door, empty-handed.

   _____

   _____

3. Forty-five minutes later, grimy and sweaty, <u>the boys were back in the car and moving</u>.

   _____

   _____

4. After all his help, <u>she owed him a few flowers anyway</u>.

   _____

   _____

5. Jeremy, <u>I'm truly touched</u>.

   _____

   _____

Extend: Read the student essay on pages 18–19 in *Write Source*. Select three sentences from the essay and write your own imitations of them.

142

Modeling a Sentence 2

Writers often write sentences with a lot of personality, rhythm, balance, and variety. They emphasize a point, a detail, a word. To learn the names for different sentence arrangements, turn to 750.1 in *Write Source*.

> **Study** the following sentences. Underline the main clause in each sentence. Then write your own version of each one, imitating the model part by part.

1. <u>An iguana hissed at us</u> as it skittered across the gravel walkway, heading for cover under a flowering bush.

   The squirrel made clicking noises as it raced across the expansive lawn, launching itself up a maple tree.

2. Since I am one of U2's biggest fans, I made sure that I was first in line for concert tickets, knowing they would sell out quickly.

3. David and Monica bounded into the room, waving their driver's licenses and whooping excitedly.

4. Despite the impending storm, the team continued its soccer practice, wanting to get in a few more plays before the rain started.

5. Drawing upon his years of experience as an instructor and businessman, he gently suggested that the staff member's efforts were inadequate for the job at hand.

Review: Sentences

Fill in the blanks to complete the following sentences correctly.

1. A simple sentence has only one _____*independent*_____ clause and

no _____ clauses.

2. A compound sentence consists of two _____ clauses.

3. A complex sentence has one _____ clause and at

least one _____ clause.

4. A compound-complex sentence contains at least two _____

clauses and at least one _____ clause.

5. _____ sentences make a statement and use a period.

6. _____ sentences ask a question and need a question mark.

7. _____ sentences make a command and use a period.

8. _____ sentences communicate strong emotion or surprise.

Write an example of the four different kinds of sentences.

1. Simple _____

_____

2. Compound _____

_____

3. Complex _____

_____

4. Compound-Complex _____

_____

_____

Pretest: Subject-Verb Agreement

> **Circle** the verb that agrees with the subject in each of the following sentences.

1. There *(are, is)* many types of athletic competitions that require intensive training.

2. Training, discipline, and hard work *(is, are)* necessary for any serious athlete.

3. The Ironman competition, whose most famous location may be Kailua-Kona, Hawaii, *(consist, consists)* of 2.4 miles of swimming, 112 miles of cycling, and 26.2 miles of running.

4. *(Has, Have)* anyone heard of an event called the Deca Ironman?

5. All participants in the Deca Ironman *(swim, swims)* 4.8 miles, *(bike, bikes)* 1,120 miles, and *(run, runs)* 524 miles.

6. Astrid Benöhr, one of the world's top athletes, *(is, are)* a world-record holder, completed this event in 187 hours in 1999.

7. What kind of a training schedule *(do, does)* a person have to follow to prepare for the Deca Ironman?

8. Surprisingly, quite a few people *(is, are)* training for the Deca Ironman.

9. Neither rain nor sleet *(keep, keeps)* them from training.

10. Each of the athletes *(is, are)* determined to train safely and sanely.

11. They *(bike, bikes)* hundreds of miles, *(do, does)* hours of strength training, and *(swim, swims)* or *(run, runs)* several hours—every day.

12. This *(is, are)* one of the sports I'd rather read about than participate in!

Subject-Verb Agreement 1

The following activity gives you practice in choosing verbs that agree with their subjects. Turn to 752.1–752.4 in *Write Source* for more information.

> **Circle** the verb that agrees with each subject in the following sentences.

1. The oldest tree in Washington County *(is,* are) dying and will have to be cut down.

2. The stately white ash *(stand, stands)* more than 70 feet high.

3. Leaves still *(sprout, sprouts)* from some of its branches.

4. But now rot *(gnaw, gnaws)* at its insides, and dead branches *(rattle, rattles)* against each other.

5. "The 250-year-old tree *(suffer, suffers)* from the complications of old age," *(say, says)* county forester Frank Smith, who adds, "It can't adapt to urban stresses."

6. But Smith *(doesn't, don't)* want this ancient tree to end up as firewood.

7. When the tree comes down, Smith *(plan, plans)* to save two or three slices of the tree's 12-foot trunk for educational purposes.

8. The rings on each cross section of the trunk *(show, shows)* the tree's actual age, and dates of historical events will be marked on the preserved slabs.

9. "This tree *(was, were)* a seedling when the Native Americans traveled through here, and luckily, they didn't step on it," *(joke, jokes)* Smith.

10. Throughout its long life, many people *(has, have)* passed this tree—maybe even George Washington, who *(was, were)* surveying forestland in the 1750s.

11. Who *(know, knows)* who rested under this venerable tree?

12. The territory *(was, were)* made a state when the tree reached its 100th birthday.

13. The old path turned into a paved road in the 1950s. Now the combination of age, heavy traffic, and car exhaust *(is, are)* putting the tree to rest.

Subject-Verb Agreement 2 (Delayed & Compound Subjects)

Single subjects need single verbs. Plural subjects need plural verbs. When a subject is *delayed*, or when the subject is compound (joined with *and* or *or*), a writer may have trouble making subjects and verbs agree. Turn to 752.1–752.4 in *Write Source* for more information.

> **Today there lurks among us an insidious threat.** (delayed subject)

> **Mercy and justice are needed in the classroom.** (compound subject joined with *and*)

> **Either Sarah or Sally is going to the dance with me.** (compound subject joined with *or*)

> **Mumps is a serious health threat again.** (plural noun but singular in meaning)

Underline the incorrect verb in the following sentences and write the correction above it.

1. The budget and the deadlines *are* ~~is~~ established.

2. The corncobs and the hay is going to be delivered here tonight.

3. This year economics or mathematics are my toughest subject.

4. There was a dozen buttons on the floor yesterday.

5. Blue and green is still my favorite colors.

6. Neither the wood chips nor the paper are catching fire in this rainy weather.

7. The team and the umpires is turning in their uniforms Friday.

8. Is the All Star players going to be named this weekend?

9. There is some players who will receive a trophy, a letter, and a plaque.

10. Camping with my brothers in the Badlands or visiting New York City with my parents were my hope for summer vacation.

11. The parents and teachers has contributed their time.

12. Parents, teachers, and students has helped write the school's bylaws.

13. Parents, teachers, or students is supposed to distribute the flyers.

14. Both my grades and my friendships needs more of my attention.

Subject-Verb Agreement 3
(Indefinite Pronouns & Collective Nouns)

When used as a subject, some indefinite pronouns (*some, most, all*) may be either singular or plural. It depends on whether the object in the prepositional phrase that comes after the pronoun is singular or plural. Also, collective nouns (*team, crowd, pair*) may be either singular or plural. It depends on whether the collective noun refers to a group as a unit or refers to individuals in the group. Turn to 754.1–754.2 in *Write Source* for more information.

> **Circle** the verb that agrees with the subject in the following sentences.

1. A few of the American colonial laws *(was,* (*were*)*)* rejected by British officials, causing resentment in the colonies.

2. "British Parliament *(has, have)* too much control over us," the colonists complained.

3. "That government *(do, does)* not have the right to rule us!"

4. "People of the colonies *(is, are)* getting weary of taxation without representation," they lamented.

5. The populace of the American colonies *(was, were)* further upset when it heard the British Parliament *(was, were)* going to tax sugar and molasses in the American colonies.

6. In Boston, citizens harassed the British soldiers, and the army troop at the Custom House *(was, were)* pleased with the attention.

7. When the Second Continental Congress met in 1775, colonial minutemen *(was, were)* battling with British forces.

8. The colonial army *(was, were)* 14,500 men strong when Washington wrote, "The men would fight very well . . . although they are an exceeding[ly] dirty and nasty people."

9. At Boston High, the faculty *(is, are)* lucky to have in its reference library a collection of letters written by famous Americans.

Review: Subject-Verb Agreement

Circle the verb that agrees with the subject in the following sentences.

1. There *(is, are)* many interesting facts about each United States president.

2. Many presidents *(was, were)* soldiers or *(was, were)* involved in wars, but only three *(was, were)* graduates of military academies.

3. Andrew Johnson and Bill Clinton *(is, are)* the only two presidents who *(has, have)* been tried for impeachment. Neither *(was, were)* removed from office.

4. Scissors *(was, were)* a handy tool for Andrew Johnson. He *(was, were)* trained as a tailor and made his own clothes. Mathematics *(was, were)* a hobby for James Garfield. News *(was, were)* publisher Warren Harding's chief interest, and medicine *(was, were)* studied by William Henry Harrison.

5. The herd of horses in George Washington's stables *(was, were)* a pampered bunch; they had their teeth brushed every morning—perhaps because Washington had no teeth of his own. Some of his many sets of dentures *(was, were)* made of cow teeth, hippo teeth, and human teeth. Others *(was, were)* fashioned from ivory and lead. Contrary to legend, none of the teeth *(was, were)* made of wood.

6. A flock of sheep *(was, were)* seen grazing on the White House lawn during Woodrow Wilson's term. The wool *(was, were)* sold to raise money for the Red Cross during World War I.

7. *(Is, Are)* anyone amazed by President Taft's bathtub? Weighing more than 300 pounds, he used a bathtub big enough for four people.

8. *James (was, were)* the first name of six presidents.

9. Here is one of those facts that *(is, are)* hard to believe. Jimmy Carter *(was, were)* the first president born in a hospital.

Pretest: Pronoun-Antecedent Agreement

Circle the correct pronoun choice in each set of parentheses in the sentences below. Then underline the antecedent or antecedents for each pronoun.

1. In 1971, portable tape <u>players</u>—the first in a long line of portable stereo systems—made *(its, (their))* debut in this country.

2. Neither the inventor nor the manufacturers could have guessed how successful *(his, their)* product would be.

3. Shizuo Takashino and other engineers used *(his, their)* expertise to create the first portable tape players.

4. Both of my sisters get upset whenever *(she, they)* can't find *(her, their)* CD players.

5. In fact, most of the people I know would not think of going on *(their, his or her)* merry way without some kind of portable music.

6. Neither Christina nor Calvin feels fully dressed without *(her or his, their)* personal music player.

7. Each of the men at the barbershop wore *(his, their)* headset while waiting.

8. All personal stereos have changed greatly since *(its, their)* introduction to the public.

9. For one thing, they are now less expensive; *(its, their)* original price was $200.

10. Most of the personal stereos today have *(its, their)* prices set under $50.

11. Carlos and Mark have made hundreds of *(his, their)* own tapes and discs.

12. One of the five CD players in our house needs *(its, their)* batteries replaced.

Pronoun-Antecedent Agreement 1

Pronouns must agree with their antecedents in number, person, and gender. Turn to page 756 in *Write Source* for more information. Also review indefinite pronouns at 754.2 and the chart of pronouns on page 704.

> **Underline** any pronoun that does not agree with its antecedent and write the correct pronoun above it.

1. Each of the 54 national parks has <u>their</u> *its* own beauty.

2. Anyone who enjoys watching whales should take their vacation in Maine's Acadia National Park.

3. None of us could believe their eyes when we spied both a humpback and a finback whale.

4. Anybody wishing to see an elk or a bison should drive their car through Yellowstone National Park.

5. Many motorists hit his or her brakes whenever one of these big beasts shows their face near a road.

6. One of the country's most extraordinary parks, known for their wild beauty, is Everglades National Park.

7. Nobody should pass up their chance to walk along the Everglades' Anhinga Trail and see the alligators, snapping turtles, and wading birds.

8. One can easily see how Big Bend National Park earned her name; the park lies on the Texas/Mexico border, where the Rio Grande makes one of his big turns.

9. Few are prepared to make his or her trek through Big Bend, because they're one of the most rugged areas in the country.

Pronoun-Antecedent Agreement 2

Antecedents joined by *and* are considered plural. Singular antecedents joined by *or* or *nor* take a singular pronoun. When one of the antecedents joined by *or* or *nor* is singular and one is plural, the pronoun must agree with the closer one. Turn to page 756 in *Write Source*.

> **Circle** the correct pronoun in each set of parentheses in the sentences below.

1. In 1804, Meriwether Lewis and William Clark led *(his,* (*their)* Corps of Discovery into the wilderness.

2. Neither the leaders nor the other men knew what to expect on *(his, their)* journey.

3. As leaders of the expedition, either Lewis or Clark could have let power go to *(his, their)* head.

4. But both Lewis and Clark listened carefully to *(his, their)* sergeants, privates, and interpreters.

5. Neither Lewis nor the sergeants would be able to communicate much with Native Americans on *(his, their)* travels, so several interpreters were hired.

6. Lewis and Clark kept notes for almost every day of the trip in *(his, their)* journals.

7. History also shows that either Sergeant Patrick Gass or Sergeant John Ordway wrote in *(his, their)* own journal.

8. Neither French trapper Toussaint Charbonneau nor his Shoshone wife, Sacagawea, knew how important *(his or her, their)* particular language skills would be to the expedition.

9. Along the way, neither Lewis nor the men could believe *(his, their)* eyes when they saw a plains grizzly.

Extend: Write three sentences about an experiment or a trip. Use *and, or,* and *nor* to join subjects in your sentences. Double-check your pronouns and antecedents for agreement.

Writers INC p. 560

Review: Pronoun-Antecedent Agreement

1   Many simple inventions have had a great impact. For example, anybody

2   who was an explorer or a soldier during the nineteenth century probably owes

3   (their, *his or her*) survival to Peter Durand. Durand, a British merchant,

4   invented the tin can. *(His, Her)* cans kept fresh foods from spoiling.

5   When Ezra Warner of Connecticut patented the first can opener in 1858,

6   *(they, it)* represented a major breakthrough. Before Warner's invention, people

7   had struggled to open *(their, his or her)* cans of food with a chisel and hammer.

8   However, a person using Warner's invention had to be very careful not to cut off

9   *(their, his or her)* fingers. Then in 1870, William Lyman introduced *(his, her)*

10   can opener, which was far less hazardous. But neither Warner nor Lyman

11   thought about powering *(their, his, her)* can opener with electricity. That

12   wouldn't happen until 1957.

13   During the 1870s, another simple product eventually made *(his, her, its)*

14   owner's name famous. William Frisbie baked and sold pies in tin plates. Over

15   the next 80 years, students from nearby Yale University ate *(their, his or her)*

16   pies and then had fun tossing the empty metal tins. When Americans turned

17   *(his or her, their, her)* eyes to the skies to look for flying saucers in the '50s,

18   Walter Frederick designed *(their, his, her)* toy flying saucer. About the same

19   time, Wham-O toy company president Richard Knerr visited Connecticut.

20   When *(he, she)* saw everyone tossing *(their, her or his)* Frisbie pie pans, *(she, he,*

21   *they)* gave the toy saucer its now-popular name.

Pretest: Sentence Combining

Combine the short sentences below into longer, more detailed sentences using the methods indicated. Add, delete, or rearrange words as needed.

- The homecoming football game started at 2:00 p.m.
- It was a special event.
- Three bands played and marched at halftime in the rain.
- By 3:00 it was pouring rain.
- The huge crowd got very wet.
- Lightning filled the air around 3:30.
- The game had to be called off.

1. Use a series. _The homecoming football game started at 2:00 p.m., the rain began to pour at 3:00, and lightning filled the air around 3:30._

2. Use a relative pronoun. _____

_____

3. Use an introductory clause or phrase. _____

_____

4. Use a participial phrase. _____

_____

5. Use a semicolon. _____

_____

6. Use correlative conjunctions. _____

_____

7. Use an appositive (or an appositive phrase). _____

_____

8. Use a conjunctive adverb. _____

_____

Sentence Combining 1

Study the groups of sentences below. Combine each group of sentences using the method indicated.

1. The film featured several big stars. It used many special effects. It had an elaborate sound track. (series)

   The film featured several big stars, used many special effects, and

   had an elaborate sound track.

2. The film grossed $400 million. It won the Academy Award for best picture. (correlative conjunctions)

   _____

   _____

3. Many scenes were improvised. The actors' skills were tested. (introductory clause)

   _____

   _____

4. The director developed his own style. It allowed actors to be creative. (key word)

   _____

   _____

5. The movie producer wanted to be historically accurate. The movie producer hired a historian to evaluate the script. (participial phrase)

   _____

   _____

6. The film was a critical success. It pleased moviegoers and reviewers alike. (appositive)

   _____

   _____

Extend: Write 10 *short* sentences about a topic you are studying. Exchange sentences with a classmate. Combine the sentences into more detailed sentences using a variety of methods.

Sentence Combining 2

Combining simple ideas into longer sentences provides variety, which is a characteristic of good writing.

> **Combine** the following sentences using the method indicated. (You may have to reword some of the sentences.)

1. **Use a relative pronoun.** Mary Cassatt was a famous American artist. She lived during the nineteenth century.

   Mary Cassatt was a famous American artist who lived during the

   nineteenth century.

2. **Use an introductory phrase and a relative pronoun.** Mary Cassatt attended art school in Philadelphia. She decided to move to Paris. This was unusual for a woman of her time.

   _____

   _____

   _____

3. **Use a semicolon.** While living in Paris, Mary Cassatt befriended many other artists. One of her closest friends was the artist Degás.

   _____

   _____

   _____

4. **Use a relative pronoun and a series.** Mary Cassatt is greatly admired for her graceful portraits of mothers with children. She is also admired for her peaceful domestic scenes. Scenes from everyday life are her most admired subjects. She is considered the most famous female Impressionist painter.

   _____

   _____

   _____

   _____

Combine the following sentences using the method you think will work best.

1. *Little Girl in a Big Straw Hat and Pinafore* is one of Cassatt's best-known paintings. Another is *Mother About to Wash Her Sleepy Child.* A third is *The Mirror.*

   _____

   _____

   _____

2. In 1893, Mary Cassatt was asked to paint a mural for the World's Fair. The World's Fair was held in Chicago. The mural was called *The Modern Woman.* This work helped make Cassatt famous in America.

   _____

   _____

   _____

3. In 1905, Mary Cassatt began to lose her vision. By 1914, she had ceased painting. In 1926, she died at the age of 82.

   _____

   _____

   _____

4. Some say that Mary Cassatt is the best-known American female painter. Interestingly, she spent most of her life abroad.

   _____

   _____

   _____

5. Cassatt worked tirelessly to help American collectors buy the finest examples of European art, by masters both old and new. She advised family, friends, and art dealers.

   _____

   _____

   _____

Review: Sentence Combining

Use the ideas listed below, rewording as necessary, to write 10 smooth-reading sentences. Tell which combining method you used to produce each sentence. (You may use an idea more than once.)

Thunderstorm Safety
- Reduce the possibility of getting hit by lightning.
- Find shelter in a substantial building.
- Small picnic shelters are unsafe.
- Rain shelters on golf courses are unsafe.
- Get off high ground.
- Move away from tall trees.
- Stay away from large metal objects.
- Get out of the water.
- Do not fly a kite or ride a bike.
- Stay in your vehicle with the windows completely closed.
- Unplug the TV and computer.
- Follow these precautions.

1. *During a thunderstorm, get off high ground, move away from tall trees, and stay away from large metal objects. (series)*

2. _____

3. _____

4. _____

5. _____

6. _____

_____

_____

7. _____

_____

_____

8. _____

_____

_____

9. _____

_____

_____

10. _____

_____

_____

Pretest: Sentence Problems

Label the problems in the following sentences. Use *F* for fragment, *CS* for comma splice, *RO* for run-on sentence, *RAMB* for rambling sentence, *WORDY* for wordiness, and *MM* for misplaced modifiers.

_____F_____ **1.** Only about 76 million Americans.

_____ **2.** In the United States in 1900.

_____ **3.** About 20 percent of the Americans had arrived, or you might prefer to say just gotten off the boat, between 1890 and 1900.

_____ **4.** William McKinley was assassinated in 1901, and then Theodore Roosevelt became president, and that was the same year that Queen Victoria died, and she had served Britain for more than 60 years.

_____ **5.** Theodore Roosevelt was a highly energetic man he liked action and the great outdoors.

_____ **6.** During Roosevelt's administration, the Panama Canal was built, the national park system was established.

_____ **7.** A rickety-looking contraption that Orville and Wilbur Wright actually flew for 59 seconds in 1903 at Kitty Hawk, North Carolina.

_____ **8.** The year 1903 was also the year of the first World Series, Boston won five games against Pittsburgh.

_____ **9.** The 1904 World's Fair was in St. Louis, and the public saw the coming wonders of the world, and electricity was one of them, and they saw airplanes and other gadgets.

_____ **10.** Consuming huge quantities of ice cream and hot dogs, the fast-food industry may have been started by the fairgoers.

Correct the problem sentences above by rewriting each, in the best possible way, on the lines below.

1. _____

_____

_____

2. _____

_____

_____

3. _____

_____

_____

4. _____

_____

_____

5. _____

_____

_____

6. _____

_____

_____

7. _____

_____

_____

8. _____

_____

_____

9. _____

_____

_____

10. _____

_____

_____

Sentence Fragments 1

A *fragment* is a group of words incorrectly used as a sentence. Because it lacks a subject, a verb, or another key element, the thought is incomplete. Turn to page 557 in *Write Source*.

> **Read** the following sentence fragments. In the space provided, write "missing a subject," "missing a verb," or "does not convey a complete thought," whichever is true. (Hint: Dependent clauses do not convey complete thoughts.)

1. while I was sleeping ___*does not convey a complete thought*___

2. the rising sun _____

3. brought the dawn _____

4. birds in the trees _____

5. sang their songs _____

6. didn't like the bird songs _____

7. pulled the covers over my head _____

8. didn't want to hear the tweet, tweet, tweet _____

9. when the birds annoyed me _____

> **Label** each group of words below as either a *sentence* or a *fragment*. Add end punctuation when needed.

____*fragment*____   1. The moon rising

_____   2. The sun rose

_____   3. When the moon was rising

_____   4. The light shining on the water

_____   5. Did the light shimmer and glisten

_____   6. As the wind whispered

_____   7. Across the water and through the trees

Extend: Use the nine fragments at the top of this page to write a paragraph. Make sure you turn all the fragments into complete sentences.

Sentence Fragments 2

Sentence fragments may sound like complete sentences, but they are missing one or more of the three essential sentence ingredients: a subject, a verb, or the expression of a complete thought. Turn to page 557 in *Write Source*.

Label the following with **S** for sentence or **F** for fragment. Use your imagination and the information in the exercise to correct the fragments.

_____F_____ **1.** The Elizabethan theater of Shakespeare's day very different from today's modern theater.

The Elizabethan theater of Shakespeare's day was very

different from today's modern theater.

_____ **2.** Often involves formal clothing and tickets purchased well in advance.

_____ **3.** Evening shows in darkened auditoriums with comfortable seating.

_____ **4.** Elizabethan plays originally were performed in open-air theaters during daylight hours—a practice some Shakespeare companies continue today.

_____ **5.** Bought tickets moments before the show for a penny apiece.

_____ **6.** The audience sitting on the ground and even on the stage.

Sentence Fragments 3

Expand and edit each fragment to create a complete sentence. Turn to page 557 in *Write Source* for assistance.

1. after I exercised in the weight room

After I exercised in the weight room, I swam laps in the pool.

2. worn-out from studying for the test

_____

_____

3. to have faith in yourself

_____

_____

4. because the room was so dark

_____

_____

5. in order to save money

_____

_____

6. editing the final draft of her essay

_____

_____

7. a popular writer

_____

_____

Extend: Use one of your sentences above as the topic sentence for a first draft of a paragraph. (Be sure your paragraph does not contain any fragments.)

    Writers INC pp. 87 and 103–104

Comma Splices

A *comma splice* results when two independent clauses are connected ("spliced") with only a comma. The comma is not enough. A period, a semicolon, a comma with a coordinating conjunction (*and, but, or* . . .), or a semicolon and a conjunctive adverb (*however, moreover, besides* . . .) must be used. The more closely related the sentences are to one another, the more appropriate it is to use a semicolon; a semicolon emphasizes this relationship. Turn to page 556 in *Write Source* for an example.

> **Fix** the comma splices in the following sentences. Use one of the methods mentioned above.

1. I really wanted to see a movie on Sunday, *but* my parents made me go weed-whack at Grandma's instead.

2. My dog hates going to the groomer, she won't get out of the car without a panting, slobbering struggle.

3. The park has picnic tables and shade canopies now, we can go there for our picnic on Saturday afternoon.

4. Thanks for finally putting away your clothes, you tracked mud up the stairs when you did it.

5. There are now environmentally safe household cleaners, they're made out of vegetable by-products.

6. I could stop at the store on my way home, you could shop for me.

7. The red splotches on my legs turned out to be a heat rash, I got it from the space heater that my teacher uses in the classroom.

8. My mom wants Karen to go to medical school, she has applied to the Arizona Institute for Disc Jockeys.

9. I pulled a muscle in my leg while moving a piano, I couldn't participate in the walkathon this year.

Extend: With a classmate, write five sentences that are "spliced" together with commas. Then decide the best method to fix each sentence.

Run-On Sentences

A *run-on sentence* is actually two or more sentences combined without the proper use of punctuation or conjunctions. Turn to page 556 in *Write Source* for an example.

> **Correct** each run-on sentence. Add a semicolon, or a semicolon with a conjunctive adverb, or a comma with a coordinating conjunction to correct some sentences. Others will need to be broken into two sentences. (Select the best method.) One sentence is correct as written.

1. Border, airport, and seaport checks become top priority when preventing the transportation of illegal drugs and explosives. Employing the help of animals has become common police policy.

2. In the battle against drugs, narcotics traffickers outnumber police officers the police have a special weapon: drug-sniffing dogs.

3. With smell receptors 100 times more powerful than those of humans, dogs such as labradors, collies, and spaniels make excellent search dogs.

4. One 12-week training course teaches a dog to recognize smells, a dog trainer, also called a handler, places a sample of the smell in a training aid made from a newspaper, a rolled-up rag, or some other object.

5. The handler hides the training aid and asks the dog to bring it back he or she rewards the dog with treats or affection for a successful retrieval.

6. The training aid changes regularly, but the sample smell remains the same the dog can recognize drugs and explosives no matter where they're hidden.

7. Eventually other scents, such as perfumes, are added this allows the dogs to find the drugs even when criminals try to disguise the scent.

8. Highly trained dogs can recognize 12 types of explosives and 4 types of drugs the dogs are never fooled by people's tricks or disguises.

Extend: Choose one of the run-on sentences above and see how many different ways you can correct it. You can use a comma and a conjunction or change punctuation, or even rewrite a clause into a phrase, but be sure to retain the basic meaning of the sentence.

Rambling Sentences

Trying to pack too many ideas into one sentence can lead to confusion. Rambling sentences often result from the overuse of *and*'s. To correct rambling sentences, remove some of the *and*'s or other conjunctions that allow the sentence to go on and on. Then fix the punctuation, and reword some parts, if necessary, to produce a better passage. Turn to page 557 in *Write Source*.

Improve the rambling sentences by removing unnecessary *and*'s. Add punctuation where necessary.

1. The Robinson family was poor but athletic, so Jackie Robinson played college sports ~~but~~ on a scholarship, and his brother, Mack, finished second in the 1936 Olympic 200-meter race, behind Jesse Owens.

2. The year 1945 proved to be a time ripe for breaking the race barrier in major-league baseball, and some sportswriters supported talented Negro League players, and minority voters applied political pressure, and the Boston Red Sox even held a tryout for minorities.

3. Branch Rickey saw racism in baseball firsthand as a college coach and later when he became president of the Brooklyn Dodgers and he set out to break the race barrier by recruiting from the Negro League.

4. A Dodger scout brought Jackie Robinson to the head office, and that is where Mr. Rickey uttered one of his most famous lines and he said, "I'm looking for a ballplayer with guts enough not to fight back."

5. The interview lasted three hours and Rickey needed that time to convince Robinson to sign with the Dodgers, and he also needed to let him know exactly how difficult it would be for a black player in a white league and Rickey said perhaps he and Robinson could open the doors of the major leagues to all players.

Review: Sentence Problems 1

> Label the types of sentence problems below. Use **F** for a sentence fragment, **R** for a rambling sentence, and **RO** for a run-on sentence. Rewrite the four sentences where lines are provided.

_____ **1.** The Korean War began on June 25, 1950, troops from North Korea invaded South Korea.

_____

_____

_____ **2.** The United Nations Security Council demanded that North Korean troops retreat the troops ignored the demand.

_____ **3.** Sixteen countries sent troops to South Korea and forty-one countries sent supplies and the United States provided most of the troops and supplies.

_____

_____

_____

_____ **4.** General Douglas MacArthur commander in chief of the Allied forces.

_____ **5.** MacArthur believed that there was no substitute for total victory and President Truman feared that MacArthur's use of "all-out measures" might lead to a third world war and he relieved MacArthur of his command in April 1951.

_____

_____

_____

_____

_____ **6.** Truce talks from July 1951 until October 1952 without a settlement.

_____

_____

Misplaced Modifiers

When a modifier is placed incorrectly, it can change or confuse the meaning of a sentence. Turn to page 558 in *Write Source*.

> **Circle** the misplaced modifier in each of the following sentences. Draw an arrow from the misplaced modifier to the word(s) it should modify. One sentence is correct.

1. The surf crested, and the beach bustled with people (over 15 feet high.)

2. Yelling "Surf's up!" Ethan grabbed his board with an excited grin and headed for the water at a full sprint.

3. Hawaii always offers the perfect waves with its tropical atmosphere for surfing enthusiasts from the mainland.

4. However, the local surfers don't always appreciate foreigners on vacation surfing at the pristine beaches.

5. Ethan steered clear of the locals paddling in another direction.

6. He finally reached the seaward side of the breaking waves with aching arms, and paddled back toward shore as a big wave approached.

7. The wave swamped Ethan and rocketed him toward the shore rolling with incredible strength.

8. Luckily, Ethan had used a special wax to prepare his board that was expensive but very sticky.

9. The breathtaking ride was the highlight of the morning and ended too soon on the neon-orange surfboard.

10. A place with top-notch beaches, Ethan expected Hawaii to have great surfing, and he wasn't disappointed.

Extend: Misplaced modifiers are often funny. Look around your classroom and briefly list some of the details you observe. Use your list to compose three "misplaced modifier jokes." Example: *The teacher has a stack of detention slips for late students sitting on her desk.*

Dangling Modifiers

When a modifying phrase or clause does not clearly and sensibly modify a word in a sentence, the result is called a dangling modifier. Dangling modifiers may be difficult to recognize in your own writing, but they are often easy to fix. Turn to page 558 in *Write Source*.

> **Underline** the dangling modifiers in the examples below and then rewrite the sentences.

1. Blasting hot water and steam 100 feet into the air, the park ranger showed us Old Faithful.

   The park ranger showed us Old Faithful blasting hot water and

   steam 100 feet into the air.

2. Three bears were spotted driving on Yellowstone National Park's twisting roads.

   _____

   _____

3. If lost in the forest, the sun can be used to determine direction.

   _____

   _____

4. Erupting every 76 minutes, our tour guide explained the origin of the geyser's name, Old Faithful.

   _____

   _____

5. Having never missed an eruption in 80 years, Yellowstone National Park attracts over a million tourists each year to see Old Faithful.

   _____

   _____

6. While exploring Yellowstone, buffalo can often be seen on the road.

   _____

   _____

Wordiness & Deadwood

The best writing is often simple writing. Wordiness and deadwood rob sentences of their clarity and simplicity without adding any significant meaning.

> **Rewrite** the sentences below, removing wordiness and deadwood.

1. To this day, today's historians are at a loss, unable to pinpoint the exact origin of the yo-yo, leaving the birth of the yo-yo a mystery.

   Historians cannot pinpoint the origin of the yo-yo.

2. It's generally accepted by most historians that the earliest records of the first yo-yos date back to ancient China, 2,500 years ago.

3. These Chinese yo-yos were basic toys with a crude design and made of common, everyday materials like wood and rock that were readily available.

4. Paintings on Greek urns from 500 B.C.E. record the historical journey of the yo-yo, depicting ancient Greeks playing with yo-yos, continuing the yo-yo's legacy.

5. As the story goes, legends speak of Philippine hunters sitting in trees using yo-yos as hunting weapons on animals below, but in these skeptical times historians dispute the accuracy of such dubious stories.

6. After all this time, throughout history, this simple toy still gives simple pleasure to millions even in this age of computer games and television.

Unparallel Construction 1

Parallel structuring is the repetition of similar words, phrases, or clauses. Inconsistent (unparallel) construction occurs when the kinds of words, phrases, or clauses change in the middle of a sentence. Turn to page 601 in *Write Source* for an example.

> **Underline** the parallel parts in the following sentences. On the lines, write the type of word or word group that is repeated in each sentence, explaining what is similar about them.

1. The driver was squeezing the steering wheel, watching oncoming traffic, and driving on the shoulder of the road.

   phrases beginning with the same verb form (-ing).

2. Rubiel likes boxing, swimming, and wrestling.

3. Annie likes Khono's optimism, Bob's cheerfulness, and Jan's helpfulness.

4. To pass this class you need to study, to think, and to remember.

5. Our team scored early, but faltered badly in the second half.

6. Taking a test is simple; passing it is hard.

7. Three of the most intelligent subhuman primates are the chimpanzee, the orangutan, and the baboon.

8. Jackie, a Chacma baboon, was probably the only monkey in history to become a corporal in the army and to earn a war medal.

Extend: Demonstrate your understanding of parallel construction by writing three to five sentences about humans and primates. Use parallel forms in each sentence, and underline each set as you did above.

Unparallel Construction 2

Inconsistent (unparallel) construction occurs when the kinds of words or phrases being used change in the middle of a sentence. Turn to page 601 in *Write Source* for an example.

Fill in the blanks with words that make sense and are parallel in form.

1. My English teacher is not only generous with his free time, but he is also _____ *generous with his praise.*

2. John had to decide whether to keep the wallet or _____ _____

3. My mom thinks rap music would be better if _____ and if _____

4. For our holiday, my family decided to _____ , _____ , _____

5. On Saturday morning I plan to _____ and _____

6. Both _____ and _____ would benefit my school.

7. To be computer literate, you should _____ and _____

8. Neither _____ nor _____ could cure Brad's bad mood.

9. Starting with the very first day of school, I found that I _____ _____ and _____ _____

Extend: Find two or three examples of parallelism in a magazine, a textbook, or another book you are reading. Share your samples with a classmate. Discuss what constructions are repeated in order to achieve the parallelism.

Review: Sentence Problems 2

Look for misplaced and dangling modifiers, wordiness, and unparallel constructions in the following sentences. Rewrite each sentence, rewording parts if necessary.

1. Falling nearly 1,430 feet, Yosemite National Park contains the highest waterfall in the United States.

   Falling nearly 1,430 feet, the highest waterfall in the United

   States is located in Yosemite National Park.

2. My dad says there are often super-perfect, wonderfully good reasons for most and maybe almost all of the school rules.

   _____

   _____

3. To be a true couch potato, you need a remote control, a couch would help, and lots of food, too.

   _____

   _____

   _____

4. Try to arrive on time and not be late.

   _____

   _____

5. Mom fixed several snacks for the children filled with healthful ingredients.

   _____

   _____

6. Buried during the avalanche, the dog rescued the skier.

   _____

   _____

7. That painting is my favorite piece in the entire gallery with the fluorescent colors.

_____

_____

_____

8. One of the things I enjoy is learning something new, but I also like to ski like I've been shot out of a cannon, and I like snooping in vintage clothing stores.

_____

_____

_____

9. Are you one of those people who take forever to say something and you just can't seem to find anyplace to stop once you get started and you take too long to make your point?

_____

_____

_____

10. The textbook had many pictures, some maps, and you could look up words in the glossary.

_____

_____

_____

11. If you could talk with a famous politician and if you could have dinner with a favorite author and if to spend a day with a movie star is your dream, which three people would you choose?

_____

_____

_____

Pretest: Shifts in Construction

Edit the sentences below, correcting shifts in construction (number, tense, person, and voice). Underline each incorrect word and write the correct word above it. *Note:* If subjects of sentences change (for example, from singular to plural), change the verbs to agree with their subjects.

1. In a recent poll, 30 percent of the people said they were happy, 60 percent said
     were   *said*   *were*
they <u>are</u> pretty happy, and only 10 percent <u>says</u> they <u>are</u> unhappy.

2. Nobody polled teens or ask him or her how they feel about the subject.

3. Of course, sad things happen, and everybody had bad days.

4. For example, when you have a cold, when a pop quiz was failed, or when you
find your favorite shirt chewed up by your dog, a person probably isn't going to
be happy.

5. Many people exercise to improve how he or she feels physically, which affects
how they felt mentally.

6. To get the greatest benefits from exercise, a person must exercise after they
properly warm up.

7. Happy people have learned to accept and to forgive herself and others.
He or she has learned to set realistic goals.

8. A happy person is often one who makes others happy, and they often have lots
of friends.

9. What goals, dreams, and wishes do you believe will make you happy when one
is an adult? What simple things make you happy?

10. I am happy when I laugh at a joke, when I read a book, when a friend is
hugged by me, or when you feel the sun on your face.

Shifts in Verb Tense 1

Verbs that describe actions happening at the same time should be kept in the same tense. Turn to 718.4 in *Write Source*.

> **Underline** the verb that shifts tense improperly and write the correction above it. The desired tense is shown in parentheses at the end of each sentence.

1. While rain fell inland, the sun *shone* is shining on the coast. *(past)*

2. The plane made an emergency landing in a valley, and the crew waits for the rescue team. *(past)*

3. When the bell rings, the students fled the classroom. *(present)*

4. I will call you so you will have known when to pick me up. *(future)*

5. The horses bolted, and the race begins. *(past)*

6. Because the days are so hot, the nights felt cooler. *(present)*

7. My writing group evaluates each piece of writing and will suggest changes. *(present)*

8. Because the doorbell rings so infrequently, Mary hurried to see who it was. *(past)*

9. Jill read the book, and she enjoys it. *(past)*

10. I did my homework and find it very difficult. *(past)*

11. My writing almost always has some sentence problems that will include fragments. *(present)*

12. If a runner does not pace herself, she will become exhausted and will lost the race. *(future)*

13. I realized you were ill, so I will call the nurse. *(past)*

14. Soon the buzzer will sound, and then we stopped working. *(future)*

15. We returned to the airport and are looking for our luggage. *(past)*

Extend: Rewrite the first two sentences in this exercise so that all the verbs are (1) present tense, and (2) future tense.

Shifts in Verb Tense 2

Verbs that describe actions happening at the same time should be kept in the same tense. Turn to page 718.4 in *Write Source*.

> **Circle** the verb that correctly avoids a shift in tense.

1. The chef went to the market and *(buys,* (*bought*)) fresh vegetables.

2. When he hit the home run, he *(tied, will tie)* the score.

3. He hits the home run, and the crowd *(goes, went)* crazy!

4. Hopefully he will hit a home run, and we *(will win, won)* the series.

5. Please clean your shoes off before you *(come, have come)* in.

6. I have cleaned my shoes, so I *(have followed, followed)* your wishes.

7. It rained gently at first, so we *(keep, kept)* the windows open.

8. You wash our clothes and *(scrub, will scrub)* the floors.

9. Keeping his head down, Syd slid into the vacant seat and *(waits, waited).*

10. The wind banged the shutters, the wolves *(howl, howled)*, and Sharien

    (felt, feels) a shiver run up and down her spine.

11. She works full-time at the bank and *(runs, ran)* a pet-walking service, too.

12. The plane takes off and everyone *(cheers, cheered).*

13. While fireworks lit up the sky, music *(fills, filled)* the stadium.

14. Play that song for your recital and *(choose, chose)* another for the concert.

15. Fabien spoke at our meeting before he *(left, leaves).*

16. I will finish my project, and then I *(went, will go)* home.

17. Ms. Kilty baked biscuits for the bake sale, but we *(eat, ate)* them.

18. They cleaned the kitchen before they *(go, went)* home.

Extend: Rewrite the last three sentences in this exercise. Change the tense of the first verb in each sentence so that the word in parentheses that you did *not* choose works.

Pronoun Shifts 1

Shifts in construction often involve the improper use of pronouns. One of the most common errors, shift in number, is moving from third-person singular to third-person plural, or vice versa. Turn to the chart on page 718, and pages 708–710 in *Write Source*.

> **A *person* needs *their* privacy.**
> (incorrect shift: *person* is singular and *their* is plural)

> **A *person* needs *his or her* privacy.**
> (correct: *person* and *his or her* are both singular)

Underline the words in the following sentences that represent a shift. Fix each shift by writing the correct pronoun above the error. (You may need to change other words to make the sentence completely correct.)

1. A pioneer needed to ration their supplies wisely.

2. After freezing nights in the mountains, many longed for his or her homes back east.

3. Everyone ought to think beyond the pay scale when they choose a career path.

4. A wise counselor once said, "Determined, focused students can blend his or her dreams with practical pursuits."

5. "Anyone can learn to do calculus," boasted Marshall, "if they work at it."

6. Jack and Todd finished his work early.

7. Both Sarah and Emily biked 110 miles to raise her share of donations for the American Lung Association.

8. Neither of Paul's parents likes their eggs poached.

9. Students are naturally very concerned about his or her environments and social conditions.

10. Anyone concerned about the future of the environment needs to do their homework and become involved.

Extend: Reword the sentences in this exercise that use *his or her*. Make the pronouns and their antecedents plural instead.

Pronoun Shifts 2

Personal pronouns are either first, second, or third person. Indefinite pronouns such as *one* are all third person. Shifting from a second-person pronoun to a third-person pronoun or noun antecedent—or vice versa—is a common error. Turn to 708.2, and the chart on page 704 in *Write Source*.

> ***You*** must drink water regularly or ***one*** will dehydrate.
> (incorrect shift: *you* is second person and *one* is third person)

> ***You*** must drink water regularly or ***you*** will dehydrate.
> (correct: both elements are second person)

> ***Athletes*** must drink water regularly or ***they*** will dehydrate.
> (correct: both elements are third person)

Underline the words in the following sentences that represent a shift in person. Fix each shift by writing the correct pronoun above the error. (You may need to change other words to make the sentence completely correct.)

1. When <u>you</u> think of what that family endured, ^{*you*} <u>one</u> can only shudder.

2. If you love to write, draw, paint, and act, people should probably not go into accounting.

3. You've entered your house and spied the present of one's dreams!

4. One naturally thinks, or hopes, that the present is for you.

5. You have to wait to find out if the present belongs to one.

6. Calculus can either stretch one's brain or burn out your circuits.

7. The soccer team knows that you can rest only after giving 100 percent to the game.

8. The students quickly realized that you needed patience to survive the class.

9. The girls went to the outlet mall because you needed new basketball shoes.

10. Most people like raw carrots better than you like the cooked carrots.

Extend: Explain in your own words what a pronoun shift is and how a writer can correct a shift.

Writers INC pp. 94, 535, and 537.2

Shifts in Verb & Pronoun Construction

The careful writer must avoid shifting (changing) from one person, tense, number, or voice to another in the same sentence. Turn to pages 752, 754, and 756 in *Write Source*.

> **Circle** the verb and pronoun shifts in each of the sentences below. Rewrite each sentence on the lines provided. Watch for shifts in person, tense, number, and voice.

1. Mark Twain grew up in Hannibal, Missouri, before he (moves) to St. Louis, New York City, and Philadelphia to work as a printer.

Mark Twain grew up in Hannibal, Missouri, before he moved to St.

Louis, New York City, and Philadelphia to work as a printer.

2. While on a voyage to Europe, Twain saw a painting of a girl named Olivia; upon seeing the picture, he falls in love with her and later was married to her.

3. The couple had four children; however, he lost his only son to a childhood disease.

4. In 1870, Twain and their family moved to Connecticut where his two most popular novels, *Tom Sawyer* and *Huckleberry Finn*, were written.

5. In the first of Twain's great novels, Tom Sawyer tricks a friend into whitewashing a fence for him and even convinced the friend to pay for the privilege.

Extend: Carefully examine a piece of your writing. Correct any shifts that you find.

Review: Shifts in Construction

> **Fill in** the blanks. This is knowledge you need in order to avoid shifts in construction.

1. Gender indicates whether a pronoun is masculine, ___*feminine*___ , or neuter.

2. List three masculine pronouns: _____ , _____ , _____ .

3. List two neuter pronouns: _____ , _____ .

4. _____ person pronouns are used in place of the name of the speaker or speakers.

5. _____ person pronouns are used to name the person or persons spoken to.

6. _____ person pronouns are used to name the person or thing spoken about.

7. The _____ of a pronoun refers to whether the pronoun is singular or plural.

8. Three examples of plural pronouns are _____ , _____ , and _____ .

9. Three examples of singular pronouns are _____ , _____ , and _____ .

10. A paragraph or longer piece of writing should use a dominant verb _____ : present, past, future, present perfect, past perfect, or future perfect.

11. A _____ shift is acceptable in a sentence (or paragraph) that states one action as happening before another action.

12. The verbs in this sentence—*I see you cleaned your room*—shift appropriately from _____ to _____ tense.

13. In this sentence—*Patrick shot the basketball and grabs the rebound before his brother had tied his shoelaces*—the three verb tenses shift from _____ , to _____ , to _____ .

14. Rewrite the sentence in question #13 to correct the shift in verb tense. _____

_____

_____

15. In this sentence—*Our new puppy is going to obedience classes and desirable behaviors are being learned by him*—the voice shifts from _____ to

_____ .

16. Rewrite sentence #15 so that the voice is consistent. _____

_____

> **Draw** one line under the personal pronouns that shift and two lines under the verbs that shift unnecessarily. Above each pronoun and verb, write the appropriate form, or cross out any unnecessary helping verb.

1   Blu-It was a "real" cattle dog. You couldn't keep him out of the cattle pens.

2   *He*
She always wants to help. One part of his name came from her breed—Blue

3   Heeler. The other part he has earned. And he starts earning his title two

4   minutes after he arrived. Although a baby himself, he felt it was his duty

5   to "herd" my little sisters whenever they are outside. He'd nip at their heels

6   to keep them in a little group. He'd get between them and the house so they

7   couldn't go inside. They have grown afraid of him. Dad made Blu a nice

8   kennel, but he eats through the wire in several hours. Mother also grew afraid,

9   so Dad makes another pen under the kitchen window. Mom could open the

10   window and drop Blu's food into her pen. It took him about three days to dig

11   out. That's when Dad says, "I guess we blew it."

Review: Sentence Activities

Write sentences following the patterns below.

1. *(subject + linking verb + predicate adjective)*

I am weary. / I feel wonderful. / I look goofy.

2. *(subject + linking verb + predicate noun)*

_____

3. *(adverb clause + compound subject + action verb + direct object + prepositional phrase)*

_____

_____

4. *(gerund phrase [subject] + linking verb + your choice)*

_____

_____

5. *(participial phrase + subject + action verb + your choice)*

_____

_____

Write an example sentence for each of the following kinds of sentences.

1. Declarative: _____

2. Interrogative: _____

3. Imperative: _____

4. Compound: _____

_____

5. Complex: _____

_____

Combine the following pairs of sentences.

1. My brother has permission to leave the house. I cannot go with him.

_____

_____

2. The sparrow hawk can travel at remarkable speeds. It can catch its prey in midair.

_____

_____

Choose the entry from column B that best describes the problem in each sentence below. Write the corresponding letter in Column A.

Column A

_____ **1.** I walked to the store because some grapes needed to be bought for the church picnic.

_____ **2.** I saw the car coming toward me and had run to the closest exit I could find.

_____ **3.** The apple tree produced very few apples, there was a problem with the pollination.

_____ **4.** If he would have been paying attention.

_____ **5.** The bear ran for the tent and it ripped open the door and grabbed the food and took off running and we were left hungry!

_____ **6.** I had to take the rope back to the store it was too short.

_____ **7.** While finding the keys to her car, the infant climbed out of the crib and down the stairs.

_____ **8.** The bright yellow sun shone on our cheerful, smiling faces as we approached the flower-flooded meadow in my friend's sun-filled yard.

Column B

a. Comma splice

b. Run-on sentence

c. Rambling sentence

d. Shift in voice

e. Dangling modifier

f. Wordiness

g. Fragment

h. Shift in tense